52 WAYS TO IGNITE
YOUR CONGREGATION . . .

WORSHIP

WAYS TO IGNITE
YOUR CONGREGATION . . .

WORSHIP

PAUL HOBSON SADLER, SR.

THE
PILGRIM
PRESS
Cleveland

To the memory of my parents,
Samuel Garner Sadler and Bobbie Ruth Sadler,
who introduced me to worship at five weeks of age

The Pilgrim Press
700 Prospect Avenue
Cleveland, Ohio 44115
thepilgrimpress.com

Biblical quotations, unless otherwise noted, are from the New Revised Standard Version of the Bible, by the Division of Christian Education of the National Council of Churches of Christ in the U.S.A., and are used by permission. Adaptations have been made for inclusivity.

Library of Congress Cataloging-in-Publication Data

Sadler, Paul Hobson, 1956–
    52 ways to ignite your congregation . . . worship /
Paul Hobson Sadler, Sr.
      p.   cm.
    ISBN 978-0-8298-1878-9 (alk. paper)
    1. Public worship.   2. Church renewal.   I. Title.
BV15.S23 2011
264–dc23   2011031465

CONTENTS

Part Three
MUSIC

Part Four
PREACHING

Part Five
LITURGY

Part Six
TECHNOLOGY

INTRODUCTION

Before we begin to discuss how to ignite your local congregation through worship, we must first establish what worship is and what worship is not. Worship is a conscious act of the human spirit, directed toward and in communion with God. It is the participatory practice of adoration of the Living God—the Creator of all things. Worship involves and engages mind, body, and spirit. It encompasses every aspect of our being and requires our participation. I have often used the phrase, worship is a verb. The very word denotes action. I once preached a sermon by that same title and at the end of the message a number of the worshippers questioned my grammatical correctness. They argued that worship, rather than a verb, is in fact a noun, but therein lies the problem. When we view worship as a place or a thing, we are negating the dynamic quality that must be present in the experience of worship. Jesus taught us and the Samaritan woman at the well this important lesson about worship in John 4:23–24, when he said, "But the hour is coming and now is here, when the true worshippers will worship the Father in spirit and in truth, for the Father seeks such as these to worship him. God is spirit and those who worship him must worship in spirit and in truth." Worship is not a construction of music, prayers, preaching, and sacraments, designed to elicit a certain response from the worshipper. That is simply liturgy: a design and plan that are constructed for the purpose of facilitating, not controlling or hindering, worship. Worship is not an event that you attend or a place to which you go. Far too many people come to think of worship in the same way as they do a concert or theatrical production. They come to be entertained. Please do not misconstrue what I am suggesting here; many people within traditional churches will argue that contemporary worship music is designed for entertainment, but I beg to differ. In fact, most of the traditional churches in America are merely providing entertainment for their congregations when they come for worship. Most of what we get in our local churches is a top ten of our favorite hymns and a sentimental liturgy that affirms what those who were raised in the church hold to be dear. But unfortunately, if we use Jesus' description in rhe fourth chapter of John's Gospel of what God wants in worship, then it is clear that there is no place for sentimentality and routine ritual in the experience of worship.

I heard that the late jazz singer Billie Holiday had a description of art that has relevance for worship. Billie said, "If it's not different each time that you do it . . . it ain't art." Worship is like this. It should be different each time that we do it, because each time that we come to worship we bring our individual experiences into the presence of God. How can you worship God the same way the day after your daughter's wedding as you do the day after you bury a loved one? If we are truly worshipping God, and not practicing some static form of liturgy, the way in which we worship must be impacted by what is going on in our lives, in the church, and in the world. Worship cannot simply be done by rote or ritual; it must issue forth from the human spirit toward God. Those of us who lived through the experience of the events of September 11, 2001, know that there is no way to come to the house of worship after the people of God have experienced such devastation and not have your worship affected by it. I have seen this done most effectively, and I have seen it dreadfully mishandled. I was once part of a congregation which experienced a devastating fire that destroyed a significant part of the church facility. On Sunday the people came with all kind of pain and all kinds of questions. However, the worship experience provided no outlet or opportunity for any of this to be addressed. The church was so stuck in its liturgy and in its goal to complete the experience in an hour that the worshippers left with the same pain and the same questions with which they entered. This is what happens when we think that worship is about liturgy and not about allowing the people of God to bask in the presence of God, for the purpose of giving God glory and of receiving the attendant blessings that come in return.

Conversely, I was a guest preacher in a local church where, during the worship experience, one of the members fell ill. The skillful and experienced pastor had all of the members join in prayer at that moment for the ill worshipper while she was attended and ultimately removed from the sanctuary for care. As the congregation was being led in prayer by the pastor, the choir director had the choir sing an old gospel standard, "Lord Do It for Me." Instead of being disrupted or disconnected, worship that day went to a whole new level of power and intensity. This is what happens when we are open to the movement of the Spirit in worship and allow the Spirit to control, not a printed order of worship.

There is a direct connection between openness to God in prayer and communication and the ability to effectively and fervently worship God. Worship that ignites a congregation is fluid and open to the movement of the Holy Spirit. It takes on a life of its own and is different each time it is experienced. Worship that becomes static ceases to be worship, because worship is in large measure affected by the spirit of the people of God when they enter into the experience of worship. Once while I was worshipping at a large congregation in a major city, the community experienced the sudden death of a beloved mayor the day before Thanksgiving. The Thanksgiving service was greatly affected by the profound sense of loss and the mourning of the community gathered for worship. Thank God, the pastor had the compassion and spiritual insight to comfort and encourage the congregation by reminding us that our future as Christians was not dependent upon the mayor who died the day before, but rather on a Savior who died nearly two thousand years ago on Calvary.

When we truly understand worship and take it seriously, it becomes an experience of transformation. When worship comes alive in the local church, extraordinary possibilities become available and accessible to the people of God, but it takes courageous and creative worship leadership to make this happen. Far too many pastors are afraid to take the risks necessary to enable their congregations to experience true worship. Fear is the enemy of the church. Where there is fear, the church cannot prosper and the people of God cannot grow. In worship, fear translates into a concern for what others will think of how we worship and into settling for playing it safe with the familiar, rather than launching out into the deep, where real, rich, and profound worship of God can occur. Only when we caste off fear can we truly engage in the powerful experience that worship can be.

In *52 Ways to Ignite Your Congregation . . . Worship*, we begin our discussion in part one with prayer—not the prayer that goes on during the experience of worship, but the prayer that is an integral part of the preparation that takes place prior to worship. In this section we discuss the importance of engaging all who participate in leading worship in the regular practice of preparatory prayer. Suggestions are offered to assist those responsible for facilitating worship in the local congregation with developing and practicing disciplined spiritual preparation prior to the worship hour. Concrete lessons are provided in how to utilize prayer as the passageway to powerful worship.

Change is one of the dynamic realities of life. Change keeps life interesting and vital. Change prevents the atrophy of the human spirit that comes with spiritual stagnation. Part 2 examines the constant need for evolution and change in the worship life of a congregation. The worship of the local church should be in a constant state of evolution. Likewise, the personal worship of the individual Christian should possess a similar character. In part 2, we discuss ways in which the local church can change its worship to address the changing spiritual needs of its worshippers. Here the reader is encouraged to see change in terms of growth rather than loss, and to embrace change in the experience of worship as necessary and healthy for the local congregation.

Music is one of the pillars of public worship. In part 3, we offer ways in which music can be effectively used to vitalize the experience of worship. We discuss concrete, simple, and proven techniques of using music to create an atmosphere of worship. Music in worship is designed to usher the worshipper into the presence of God. Psalm 150 suggests that everything that breathes should praise God. Our worship should involve every fiber of our being and every aspect of our experience. As our text continues we discuss the use of instrumentation in worship and ways in which effective use of instruments in worship can enhance and enliven the worship experience. We discuss how the use of instrumentation can engage people of all ages in participating in worship and in playing a vital role in bringing new life to the worship experience. Utilizing the suggested music methodologies will transform the worship of your local church.

Pivotal to any text on worship is a conversation on preaching. How we communicate the gospel has a profound effect on the experience and power of worship in the local church. In part 4, our discussion focuses attention not on style but rather encourages authenticity and transparency in the preaching ministry of the church. We pay particular attention to finding one's voice in preaching and to theological integrity in the preaching enterprise. Here the pastor is encouraged to explore the depths of his or her creative spiritual reservoir so that preaching becomes an authentic expression of what God is doing in the heart, mind, and soul of the preacher.

In part 5 we discuss the place and effectiveness of liturgy in the twenty-first-century church. We examine the concept of "living liturgy" in the worship life of the local congregation.

Most importantly, we explore the need for change in the liturgy of many churches today, to be attentive to the changing contexts of contemporary worshippers. We offer to those who design the framework for corporate worship the tools to take their liturgy to a whole new level of vitality and help those charged with constructing liturgy to develop a freedom in the Holy Spirit that will enliven the experience for all who worship.

Catholic and Anglican Christians have long understood the value of the aesthetic to the public worship space. Here we discuss how less liturgically oriented churches can take advantage of the beauty of place and space in the worship experience. We examine the value of robes/worship attire for those leading worship and the adornment of the worship space in facilitating and creating the setting for worship. Here examples are given of worship space that works and of worship space that does not. We also provide the reader with easy ways to transform existing worship spaces into settings that can encourage the worshipper to encounter the living God.

The last section, part 6, of 52 *Ways to Ignite Your Congregation . . . Worship*, explores the usefulness of technology in worship. Here we discuss the power of sight and sound that technology can bring to the context of worship. We explore the benefits that technology has brought to the experience of worship and how easily those benefits can be shared with the worshipping congregation. There is no limit to what can be achieved when technology is used effectively.

My hope is that this book helps you to see worship in a new and different way. In so doing, you will become engaged in the enterprise of facilitating worship in some new and very exciting ways. If you embrace the concepts offered in this book, you will experience the power and the blessings that come when a congregation is ignited in worship. The instructions within these pages are designed to transform the experience of worship in your local church, so do not expect as you practice these suggestions that your church and its worship will remain the same. In fact, I will be greatly disappointed if this text does not disrupt the ways in which you now view worship and cause you to see it in a whole new way. My prayer is that after reading *52 Ways to Ignite Your Congregation... Worship,* worship for you will never be the same.

Part One

PRAYER

Prayer is the key to connecting with the power within,
seeking a deeper connection with God
and members of the congregation.

Pray

Prayer is a vital and necessary component of worship. However, far too many pastors and worship leaders/facilitators have missed this one important fact: the prayer that takes place before worship is equally as important as that which occurs within the context of a public worship experience. Prayer is the foundation of the Christian life, so it stands to reason that prayer would also be foundational to Christian worship. In fact, it is the first step toward a vital ministry of worship in the church. Without prayer we are primarily acting on our own impulses and insights. Prayer ushers us into the presence of God, and when we pray about worship, our prayers move the heart of God toward us and move us toward the heart of God. This prepares the soil of the spirit to enter into sincere heartfelt worship.

When we pray about worship, we are seeking God's will that we might really worship God in spirit and in truth. When we acknowledge that true worship is what God desires, our worship can be freed from the routine rituals that have little real value to worship other than their familiarity. True worship should be like looking at a work of art. Each time that you see it, you see something different, because as we join in public worship, each of us brings with us our own unique set of life experiences and our differing relationships with God the Creator. As we pray about worship, God works to bring those experiences together into one common place and time, in the one Spirit.

The apostle Paul teaches us in his first letter to the Corinthians that "there are varieties of gifts but the same Spirit." As we come to the experience of worship, each person brings varied and different gifts. As we seek to lead and enable in the local church, we must pray that, out of the cacophony of our experiences and the diversity of our gifts, God would create a symphony that would glorify and honor God. We must never forget this one important fact: the purpose of worship is to glorify God.

Far too many in the traditional church have looked at worship as simply a time to be inspired, uplifted, and comforted. There is a serious problem with this concept of worship. Worship cannot and must not ever revolve around the needs of the worshipper. This type of worship misses the true meaning and intent of what worship is supposed to be. The purpose of worship is to glorify God and to lift before the people the suffering and sacrifice of God's son Jesus Christ. When we do this, people are drawn to God's church and to a real relationship with God. This relationship is not based on getting individual and personal needs met in worship. Instead it is based on worshipping and serving a living God, and blessings to the worshippers issued from their worship of God. This kind of religion manifests itself horizontally in how we treat and care for one another, particularly the least among us. You cannot truly enter into the presence of God in worship without facing God and yourself. This encounter is transforming, but the transformation begins in prayer.

Genuine worship can be experienced when we surrender to God in prayer our need to control worship. When worship is alive and vital, God is in control. As a worship leader/facilitator your job is to help create the atmosphere in which worship can occur. When you do this, worship becomes true adoration of a God who is worthy to be praised, and the by-product is phenomenal blessing for the body of Christ.

So how do you develop the discipline of praying for and about the worship of your church? Begin at the beginning: in the planning process. Pray over every aspect of your worship service. Pray about the music and the preaching. Pray about the welcome and the invitation. Pray about the atmosphere and the setting of worship. Living in Cleveland, Ohio, I frequently find myself praying about the weather. It seems as though it would not be as important as it is to the worship of God, but it is. Many Christians look at the weather forecast before they get dressed for church on Sunday, not to determine what they will put on, but to determine, before they get dressed, whether they are going to church at all. The one thing that can counteract all of these traditional practices when it comes to worship is for the people of God to be engaged in fervent praise and adoration to God. I saw this manifested when I lived in Chicago many years ago.

My first winter in Chicago, the large church where I was serving as an associate Pastor scheduled a 7:30 a.m. Christmas service. I was sure that only the righteous remnant would show up. On Christmas morning when I arose, the temperature was twelve degrees below zero. I expected to find a sparsely populated sanctuary when I made it to the house of God on Christmas day after driving through the barren streets with ice on the inside of my windshield. But to my surprise, at that early hour and at that frigid temperature, when I arrived at church at about 7:15 a.m. the parking lot was full, and when I entered the sanctuary every seat was filled and people were standing along the walls. I was shocked and amazed, but I learned something about worship that day. That morning, eight hundred people showed up in the most unfavorable of conditions to worship God. Church was like this every Sunday, but what I had failed to realize was that this church had been taught through the preached word of the importance of the birth of Jesus. Worshipping God on Christmas Day was not only important to this congregation's spiritual identity, it was necessary. When worship is alive and vital, people not only come but they also invite others to share this blessed experience with them.

Many years ago I asked my mentor, Dr. Jeremiah A. Wright Jr., the key to growing a vibrant congregation, and his answer was simple: music and preaching. I later found out something more about that which empowered worship in the church that he served for more than thirty years, and that was that he spent hours of prayerful preparation for what happened at the Sunday worship hour.

I had the opportunity to interview a pastor of a large New England congregation when I was writing an article on prayer. I have never forgotten something that he shared with me. He spoke of the many prayer groups that he had started within his church. When I asked about his personal prayer life, I was surprised to learn that the second largest amount of time that he spent in prayer, after praying for the members of the congregation, was the time that he spent in prayer for the worship of the church. How much time do you spend in prayerful preparation for what happens when the people of God come to worship? Rev. Clay Evans is famous for singing "It Is No Secret What God Can Do." However, my experience working with churches in mainline denominations tells me that God's desire and willingness to respond to our prayers could be the best-kept secret in the Christian church today.

Rev. Otis Moss III frequently says that "there can be no preaching without praying." From all of this, we can surmise that prayer plays a vital role in the worship life of the congregation, and if you want to ignite your congregation through worship then prayer is the place to begin.

Fast

Fasting is one of the spiritual disciplines that gives us greater access to the power of God, when coupled with fervent prayer. Fasting is intentional self-consecration through refraining from eating certain foods, or food in general, for a set period of time. Fasting opens the human spirit to hear more clearly from the Spirit of God. It enables us to more clearly discern the will of God through prayer and meditation. Whenever I have been faced with a major decision in my ministry, I have always set aside a time of prayer and fasting so that I would be able to determine the direction in which God would have me go.

In worship it is important to know what God desires to communicate to the body of Christ. As a worship leader I have always sought to create a tapestry of worship through liturgy, music, prayer, and preaching that was knit together with the thread of the Holy Spirit. This is only possible when discernment of the will of God for the people of God takes place, and that discernment can only happen when the worship leaders are connected to the Holy Spirit. We often take our connection to the Holy Spirit too lightly.

Having grown up in a highly liturgical church, where all worship was scripted in advance and routine, I had no experience with seeking the creative power of God for direction in worship. However, once I became responsible for designing a framework for fresh worship on a weekly basis, I had to seek a source that was higher than scripted liturgy to bring new life to the worship service each week. That source was the Holy Spirit.

When you are trying to ignite your worship service, you must first be ignited. If there is one thing about dying congregations and desperate pastors that drives me crazy, it is that they grab on to every new book and new philosophy of church growth, much like the first-century Greeks who were always looking for the next new thought or new wave to come on the scene. The apostle Paul said that they were blown about by every wind of doctrine. I hope that you will understand this text not as a new way of doing worship or enlivening the church, but rather as an affirmation of the biblical insights and principles about worship that most of us know, but so often ignore. I wholeheartedly believe, as the United Church of Christ asserts, that God is still speaking.

What I also believe, however, is that God has been infinitely clear in God's Word, the Bible, how God desires to be worshipped. If our desire is to be obedient to the word and will of God where worship is concerned, then we must draw closer to God. This will enable us to hear more clearly what God wants and expects of us. One important way to draw near to God is through fasting.

Fasting enables you to seek that deeper connection to the Holy Spirit and to God's will that will help you to ignite your worship experience with the dynamic power of God's Spirit. I have had the privilege of worshipping in churches of many cultures across this nation, and I have found one common thread in all of the churches that were alive and vibrant. That thread is the clear sense that worship was being led and empowered by the Holy Spirit. It did not matter what the denomination was or its theological bent. What did matter was that those who were leading worship had a connection to the Holy Spirit. Fasting is one important way to seek and sustain that connection. When we consciously sacrifice food as an act of spiritual consecration or setting oneself aside for discernment of God's will, it opens a direct line of communication with the divine source of power, guidance, and direction.

There are a number of ways to fast that I think are important to share at this point. The most common type of fasting in the Bible was the absolute fast from all foods with the consumption of water only. In contemporary times, fasting has evolved to become more accessible to people with differing health conditions. Today, many Christians observe fasts that include refraining from certain foods such as meats, flour, and sugar or solid foods. One form of fasting that is rising in popularity within the contemporary Christian church is the Daniel Fast. This fast finds its essence in Daniel 10:3, where Daniel refrained from all pleasant food for twenty-one days. Hence, the Daniel Fast normally lasts for twenty-one days. Individuals who opt for this type of fasting refrain from meat, sugar, flour, and all processed foods, which means any foods containing added chemicals.

The particular benefit of the Daniel Fast is that most doctors would approve it for their patients suffering from specific dietary-related or health disorders. However, as always, if you are under a doctor's care, check with your doctor before starting any major or long-term dietary changes. For more information, visit the Daniel Fast Web site: *www.daniel-fast.com.*

I asked members of our congregation many times to join me in a twenty-one-day Daniel Fast. Those who took the fast seriously, praying fervently for the twenty-one days, understood it as a spiritual journey and discipline. They experienced phenomenal blessings as a result. Those who saw it as a diet simply lost weight, which most quickly regained following the fast. However, many people's lives were changed forever as a result of the fast. This is the power of fasting. When done sincerely, fasting yields lasting and often lifelong results. When I first experienced the Daniel Fast I could not imagine how I could give up sugar in my diet and processed foods. After all, what could I eat for lunch other than fast food and soda? After two weeks without sugar, though, my body began to adjust to life without chocolate donuts, and I began to feel as though I could give up sugar forever. And that's what I did! I have returned only fish and dairy to my diet, opting for a food plan similar to that of food addicts in Recovery Anonymous. What is most important is the clarity of thought, focus, and discernment that this discipline afforded me, when coupled with faithful and fervent prayer.

If your desire is that your worship be ignited with the power of the Holy Spirit, then fasting is an important way to begin this process. As you fast, focus your prayers on that which you desire. If your desire is to see new life in a failing congregation where worship is simply routine ritual, monotonously repeated, then fasting is not merely an option, it is a necessity. What you are really asking God for has very little to do with music, liturgy, or preaching. What you are asking God to do is transform human lives. What really brings about change in worship is when people's lives have been changed, because people worship the way they live. If people are totally surrendered to God, then that's the way that they worship. If Christ is first in their lives and in their commitments, then that will be reflected in the way in which they worship. You will not be able to revive a dying congregation or lifeless worship experience without turning to God to transform the worshippers who come Sunday after Sunday. Once you pray for God to transform the worshippers, the next thing that you must do is to pray for clear and concise direction from God as to what God wants you to do to help facilitate a worship revitalization in your church. Fasting helps you get this kind of clarity in your prayers. Know what you want from God on your fast, though. Be clear and direct in what you ask. If you fast long enough and faithfully enough, God will give you what you ask as long as it is in God's will. Many of us set out on the path of spiritual discipline with a plan for God. We know what we want God to do and are prepared for God to act in accord with our desires and plans. This, however, is a faulty path to spiritual insight and direction. We must be open to what God wants for us and for the church in order for us to receive our marching orders for our next steps.

Remember this basic principle in prayer and fasting: if you knew what needed to happen, you would have already done it, and if you, in and of yourself, had the ability to fix your worship service or your church, surely you wouldn't be spending time reading this book—you would be doing it. We must come to the spiritual discipline of fasting with deep humility, acknowledging that we do not know what to do next and that we need God's guidance and direction to move forward effectively. Once that is acknowledged, you can then be open to the movement and leading of God's Spirit and act on the things that you see and hear. I use the term "see" because much of the guidance that we get from God comes in visions and pictures that God places in our minds. Elizabeth Alves, in her book *Becoming a Prayer Warrior*, describes these images as pictures in the theater of the mind. This is a very apt description of how God speaks to us and shares information and insight with us. It is difficult for these images to come to you while watching television or surfing the Internet. The most fertile soil for the voice of God is a place of privacy and silence, where you can hear God's voice and see God's visions without distraction. In these places and times,

God can speak profoundly to you about the things, people, situations, and issues about which you should pray and act.

When focusing your fast on igniting your worship, you must diligently pray for God to have complete control of the worship service. You must pray for God's will to be done in worship, and you must pray for God to infuse the worshippers with the Holy Spirit. Fasting is a way to enable you to discern what God would have you do in the worship of your church. It is a powerful tool for igniting your congregation and for deepening your spiritual life in general.

Be Open to the Leading of the Holy Spirit: Learn to Listen

Listening for the voice of God, the Holy Spirit, to lead you in worship is a key element in truly igniting your congregation. Often we become subservient to the liturgy of worship, rather than allowing the liturgy to be the instrument of the Holy Spirit to help orchestrate our worship of God. This is where our definition of worship becomes extremely important. When we see worship as a place that we go or as a thing that we observe, then our worship can never truly have life. Worship is the action of adoration toward God. It is consciously expressing our love, gratitude, and admiration for God as a body of believers in a public setting. This practice cannot be effectively accomplished without openness to the Holy Spirit on the part of the worshipper and especially on the part of those who lead worship.

Most Christian churches have become so enslaved by the order of worship and the clock that we come to believe that God can only move during a set period of time and according to what has been printed in the worship bulletin. This understanding of worship is a primary roadblock to allowing our worship to be ignited with the Spirit of God. I have been in worship services that lasted fifty minutes where all kinds of transformation took place and the worshippers were spent as if they had been worshipping for hours. I have also been in services of worship that lasted for hours and the worship leaders literally had to tell the worshippers to go home. Conversely I have been in long and short worship experiences that were so dreadfully dead and so woefully void of the presence and power of God that they were intolerable. The key to powerful, meaningful, and memorable worship is the presence of the Holy Spirit in the worshipper and in the worship experience. Remember that the Holy Spirit does not dwell in sanctuaries or in other worship spaces. The Holy Spirit dwells in the worshipper. We bring the Spirit to the house of worship, and the Spirit leaves with us when we go. If those who come to worship come without the power and presence of the Holy Spirit dwelling on the inside, then true worship is impossible.

Openness to the leading of the Holy Spirit begins in the planning process. Those who are charged with planning and leading worship must be led and guided by the Holy Spirit. They must surrender to God's will and be willing to sacrifice their desire to accomplish a certain goal in worship, for the will and purpose that God desires to be accomplished in worship. When planning worship, the first and most important step is prayer. When we pray we open ourselves to receive what God has for us. When we listen quietly and intently, God speaks to us and shows us the vision and the plan that we should follow in our services of worship. That vision is often evolving and may change as you draw closer to the worship experience. This is based on two things: experience and inspiration. Throughout the course of any given week, many things happen in the life of a church. These may be things that happen in the church directly, in the community, or in the world. Depending on their direct or emotional impact on the church membership, these events can influence the worship experience significantly. The worship leader thus must maintain sensitivity to the leading of the Holy Spirit and remain prayerful, so that needed ministry can take place within the context of worship.

The next area in which you need to be open to the leading of the Holy Spirit is in the preparation phase of worship. All involved in worship preparation, including musicians, choir directors, choir members, and worship leaders, need to understand the purpose, focus, and direction of worship. Knowing and understanding biblical themes and contexts is also important. Most important, all involved in worship must be of one accord. The harmony and unity in the chancel will be visible and will transfer to the pews. This harmony must be built through prayer, fellowship, worship, and the study of God's Word together.

My experience working with churches has taught me the importance of having unity of purpose among the leadership. When there is disunity in the leadership, God's purpose and plan for the church can be thwarted or derailed. When it comes to the worship experience, this is of particular importance. Such unity, however, is often not present in many of our more traditional churches. In fact, the services of worship and those who provide leadership for them are often the source of much contention within the body of Christ. This is largely because individuals forget or ignore the fact that worship is not and should not be focused on the worshipper but rather on the One being worshipped. I have so often said that many come into the doors of our churches Sunday after Sunday with no thought or concern about worshipping God in Spirit and truth. Instead, their primary goal is to have an experience that is comforting and sentimental, with complete disregard for the God whom we claim we come to worship. We can change this flawed paradigm if we would simply begin to teach and model for our congregations what real authentic worship is. The teaching aspect is most important.

Most church members come to worship with much baggage. This baggage comes from every church that they have ever belonged to and every worship experience that they have ever attended. This baggage was often packed in childhood when we developed certain attitudes about the church and those inside, and now that we have become adults our baggage has remained unexamined. Many worshippers judge their church's worship (and its leadership, for that matter) in comparison to the church where they grew up or the last church they attended. On the other hand, many worshippers have no previous experience with worship and find it confusing and pointless. This is why we must seek the leading of the Holy Spirit in worship. As the Holy Spirit guides the worship experience it becomes a time of transformation in the presence of God. Some people know all of what I have shared and resist this understanding of worship largely because they cannot control it. There is a genuine fear in the hearts and minds of many of being out of control. These are the worshippers who have yet to experience the blessing of surrender. When we surrender to the Holy Spirit in worship, our experience of worship rises to a whole new level and our communion with God in worship reaches yet unexplored vistas. We must be conscious of all of these diverse experiences in planning and preparing worship so that with the guidance and direction of God's Spirit we can all bring our differing and unique gifts to the house of worship with the intention of honoring the Living God.

Pray with Your Choir Director

Your choir director is also a leader of worship. She or he brings the power to create a worshipful space through the choice of songs for the choir and for the congregation. As I've learned, the choir director is an important person in helping to set the tone for worship, bringing creativity, insight, and spirituality to the worship experience. By understanding the purpose, focus, and direction of the service, she or he can help to select songs, hymns, and anthems that support and enhance worship. The pastor and choir director should be of one accord and grounded in the Scripture and theme of worship before the music is chosen. Together, pastor and choir director can share ideas about what kinds of songs should be included in the worship service. The choir director can teach the choir the biblical basis and message of the songs that are included as well as a sense of how the songs flow and support that Sunday's theme.

Do not underestimate the power of congregational singing! The choir director and worship leaders can teach songs to the congregation during worship and even before the worship service begins that will enliven and empower the experience of worship. I have witnessed this in many churches and especially in the large urban church where I served many years ago as associate pastor. Worshippers often arrived early for services to ensure they had seats in the main sanctuary. Many would arrive up to an hour before service began. The choir director would introduce new songs—explain who wrote the song and why it was written—and share with those in the sanctuary why this particular song was relevant to the congregation and that Sunday's worship. The choir director then led the congregation in singing the song—verse by verse. After singing several times through, the congregation was more comfortable singing the new song within the context of the worship service. When the time came for the congregation to sing the song, they were ready; they saw how the song fit into the larger context of the service and were able to sing with joy, gusto, and conviction. The choir director was empowered and valued as an important part of the service. When the pastor and choir director have a relationship that is built on prayer, there is no question that the choir director has the support and respect of the pastor. This prayer relationship helps to create a suitable space for God's people to encounter the Divine.

Prayer with the choir director should include asking God to have complete control of the worship experience in spite and because of what is planned. It should focus on God being glorified in our worship, above all else. Their prayer time should include seeking an openness to the movement of the Holy Spirit at all stages of the planning and the implementation of those plans in worship. You and your choir director need to ask God's blessings upon the service and make yourselves available to the movement and anointing of the Holy Spirit. I was constantly amazed at how well Rev. Dr. Jeremiah A. Wright Jr., pastor emeritus of Trinity United Church of Christ, and Trinity choir director Dr. Jeffrey P. Radford worked together to create a space for authentic, energized, and vital worship each Sunday. Before the choir was assembled for rehearsal, the pastor and choir director prayed together, planned together, and determined what music best suited that Sunday's theme. It helped that Dr. Wright is a musician in his own right—composing and playing music and writing lyrics. But even in situations where the pastor is musically challenged, having a prayer relationship with a gifted choir director, who not only shares your space but your faith as well, will be an invaluable asset in igniting worship. Together you can create a space for the congregation to worship in ways that are authentic and true.

I was truly blessed in the first church where I served to have as minister of music one of the most gifted musicians in our community. He not only directed our church choir but also a high school choir and a large community choir based on a college campus. Arphelius Paul Gatling III was a pastor's dream of a minister of music. He was trained in classical choral music and rooted in gospel music, and he loved each with an equal passion. He enabled our choir and congregation to be exposed to all kinds of phenomenal worship music and helped the worship of our church to grow in extraordinary ways.

When our church would host its annual service of song at the eleven o'clock worship hour during Advent, the church would be packed to the rafters with those who came to experience this unique yet powerful kind of worship. But this was what we came to expect each Sunday. Most importantly Arphelius Gatling was rooted in the gospel of Jesus Christ. His musical expressions were the manifestation of the power of God that was moving on the inside and that he gave vent to each Sunday in worship.

Each local church is different, but I have been blessed to serve with some tremendously gifted and anointed musicians in my pastoral settings. In a much smaller church I served, where resources were far more limited, I truly learned the power of praying and asking God for what you need. In this church there was a classically trained and rather mature choir director, who had no interest or love for anything contemporary. Since I consider myself a post-Black Power generation baby boomer, existing without gospel music in worship was simply not going to work for me. It is too much a part of my identity as an African American and as a Christian.

When I first graduated from college and was still finding myself, preministry, I purchased a car: a 1969 Chevy Nova with only AM radio. I don't like listening to AM radio because of its lack of diversity and poor signal, but the one channel that I liked on AM was the gospel station. So I locked my radio on it and listened to it every day. It was ultimately the message of the gospel music on that AM radio station that influenced me to surrender my life to Christ. Thus, for me, gospel music has always been an important part of the way in which I worship God.

My elder organist, though, wasn't having it. I began to pray for God to send a musician who would be open to all types of worship music, and God did just that. The problem was that he lived forty miles away in another city and the trip on Sunday was a challenge, and beside that, the church could not afford to pay him what he was worth. I resolved this by offering for him to spend Saturday nights in our guest room in the parsonage. This worked really well—so well that Saturday night turned into Sunday night, Monday, and Tuesday as well. Our relationship became like Paul and Silas. We prayed and labored together to build and revitalize the church.

Eventually my children started calling him "uncle" and when I left that church to move on to another ministry he rented the parsonage from the church and ultimately married and raised a family there. This gifted young musician drew scores of talented and anointed young singers to our church and enhanced our worship ministry exponentially. Here's the point: I prayed and God sent me what I needed, but I had to possess the flexibility to do what was necessary to facilitate the blessing.

Pray with the Choir

Choir members must be empowered as worship leaders to offer their gifts to God. They should be reminded that what they do they do *not* do for fame, attention, or their own ego needs. Their voices are gifts from God, and singing is their response to God's gift. The music of the church is one of the most important tools available to the church for evangelism. The choir not only offers their music as gifts but also they lead the congregation in singing praises and honor to God. When possible, attend choir rehearsals and pray before any music is distributed or songs sung. Share with choir members the Scripture and theme for the upcoming Sunday.

Tell the choir why the texts and theme are important in the life of your church. Thank the choir director for helping to select the music for the service and for being the instrument of God to teach this music to the choir. Take the time to share with the choir how the songs fit into the overall worship experience, sharing with them the biblical undergirding and spiritual message in each selection. By doing this, you enable each choir member to see their individual part in helping to make the music of worship a vehicle through which the Holy Spirit can move in a transformative way on the hearts of the worshippers.

Then, pray with your folks. Ask for God's anointing on the gifts that they bring, on their voices and their lives. Be sure to express gratitude to God for their faithfulness and for their commitment to sharing their gifts with the congregation. Bless their rehearsal time and let them know how much you appreciate the sacrifices they make in order to serve in the choir.

On Sunday morning, be sure to pray with the choir before worship begins. Again, thank them for their service, introduce any special guests, and highlight special aspects of that Sunday's service. Ask God to bless and keep each member, to anoint and fill them with God's Holy Spirit so that their singing is authentic, heartfelt, and powerful. Let your prayer time be spontaneous, asking God to help all render their best service for worship. This important and vital step will help to ignite worship and move your congregation to a new place in God, and should not be minimized or ignored. Failure to take seriously the ministry of prayer with your choir will hinder the growth of the ministry of music and the important role they play in leading the congregation in worship.

It is also important to help the choir bond together in a unity of worship that God uses in a unique way each Sunday. I have always recognized the value of the choir getting together for fellowship outside of the church. Barbeques and holiday parties are important to the bonding that needs to take place in order for the choir members to see themselves as a unit of worship. In the military they would be seen as a battalion with a lieutenant who provides guidance and leadership. Once this bonding takes place, undergirded by prayer and solid training, there is no limit to what the choir can accomplish as a unit of worship.

Pray with Your
Worship Leader(s)

All who are chosen to participate in worship leadership need to feel empowered and supported in their ministry of service. One of the most stressful acts for many people is public speaking. Even the most accomplished persons may find themselves feeling insecure and nervous when asked to participate in public worship—all the more reason for the pastor to pray with them. Ask God to strengthen each participant for the tasks ahead. They will feel supported and may find that they have gifts they have been hiding because of fear.

For years I have asked all worship leaders—greeters, ushers, liturgists, deacons, praise leaders, and worship leaders—those lifting the offering, those reading Scripture, and those offering prayers—to meet with me before worship for a time of prayer and brief sharing. It's an opportunity for us to gather, greet one another, and get on the same page before we move into worship. Here, we have the chance to share the latest information about any aspect of our life together—who may have gone into the hospital, who may have been released from the hospital, any emergency situations, any adjustments that need to be made because persons could not honor their commitment to lead that day, how to recognize special guests. This time allows us to see each other, clarify assignments, and pray together for a Spirit-filled and meaningful worship experience. Prayer takes the focus off of us and places it where it belongs—on God!

Prayer reminds us all that we are serving together to glorify God and to set the tone for worship. Worship leaders should be bathed in prayer before the worship service begins. This helps all to swallow those butterflies and offer their best service to God and to the congregation. In fact, praying for all who lead worship helps to remove the element of discomfort for all who are called to a time of leadership in the Holy of Holies. But let us not forget that preparation is a necessity for all who lead God's people in worship. We do a disservice to God and to God's people when we show up unprepared, as if anything that we do will be alright because it's the church. In fact, our reverence for God should cause us to believe just the opposite. We should give our best service to God. If we are called on to make a presentation at our job we would not think of showing up late or unprepared. How then can God, the Creator of all things, not be accorded the same honor and respect? When we are prepared, it takes much of the anxiety out of what we are called to do before the people of God. It also models the appropriate way to lead worship.

Coming together as one in prayer prior to leading worship helps to set the spiritual tone for the ministry that each worship leader is called to do. It unites the worship leaders into a cohesive unit and helps each to see their role as equally valued. Most important, God is honored when we take the time to seek God's presence and blessing on all that we do as we go to God in prayer.

Pray with Your Musicians

I once heard a well-respected preacher end his sermon with this short litany: "little prayer, little power; some prayer, some power; much prayer, much power!" I have found these words to be true, especially as they relate to vital worship. And music is a big part of vibrant worship. It makes sense to pray with the musicians. Uninspired musicians produce uninspired music. We want the music to be praise-filled and authentic. Prayer, listening to the Holy Spirit, and being open go a long way in creating music that moves people. At the end of an anointed musical selection, people feel that they have been in the presence of the Divine. It is easy for musicians to feel that they are performers or merely hired staff if they are not involved in the inner workings of what the worship service is all about. When musicians are engaged in prayer time with the other worship leaders and when you take the time for individual prayer with them, the difference in their commitment and their ministry will be obvious.

Take the time to get to know the people who are integral to facilitating worship in your church. Whether you have one organist/pianist or a band, having a prayer relationship with your musician(s) helps to breathe new life into the experience of worship.

Do not neglect praying with your musicians. Their role in worship is significant, and they can make or break a service.

Have an Overnight Lock-In Prior to Worship

Have some set-apart time with all those who participate in worship—a time for prayer, fasting, singing, and testifying. You may want to schedule an overnight lock-in at the church from time to time. This event provides an opportunity to connect with each other and to the Divine. It is a time away from the distractions of life—phones, texts, email, Facebook, and Twitter—and a time to focus on God and what God requires of those responsible for worship. It is easy to burn out from the stresses of creating weekly services and additional services that are a part of congregational life. Weekly rehearsals can become monotonous and learning new music tedious. Even the occasional personality conflict can test the patience of the most faithful choir member. But taking the time to be with one another in an atmosphere dedicated to seeking God's will for our ministry of music and the church's worship can yield tremendous dividends.

The first time I proposed this to my worship leaders—choir director, choir members, and musicians—I expected a great deal of push back. I could hear them now: "Why do we have to stay overnight? Why can't we just have a meeting like we always do? What do you expect to accomplish by such a thing? I want to sleep in the comfort of my own bed!" I was shocked to find out that they were all on board. For them, the lock-in was like a retreat—a time to focus on God and to remember why they were engaged in this kind of ministry. For many it was a first-time experience. For others it reminded them of their childhood, when they attended youth lock-ins at the church in which they grew up. I have experienced many lock-ins over the years: with the youth of the church, confirmation retreats, and adult prayer lock-ins at which the adult members of the church prayed in the sanctuary all night. In all of the lock-ins I have experienced, the results were always positive.

You might be pleasantly surprised to learn that your leaders also want some time away—to reflect, meditate, and bond with each other and with you. Try it!

Part Two

CHANGE

The only constant in life is change,
and congregations are always dealing with change.
There may be changes in leadership (ordained and laity),
in membership, in the community surrounding the church,
and certainly in the wider society.
Let's make change happen,
rather than work against it!

Try Something New

Sometimes we find ourselves in a rut. We keep doing things because it's the way we've always done them. We don't take the time to think about why we do what we do. Even less do we ask if what we are doing is relevant anymore. Do something different in the worship service: change the worship time, change the music, change the worship space, change the order of worship—change *something*.

Most congregations have a time during the worship service, usually near the middle for announcements and updates. For a change, try making the announcements before the worship service starts. Most folks gather in the sanctuary ten to fifteen minutes before worship. Make the announcements at that point, before the prelude and call to worship.

If you always change the time for worship during the summer, try keeping the standard times. One pastor I know jokingly says that everyone goes on summer vacation except God!

If you don't already, add a mission moment to the service to share with the congregation how mission dollars are spent and why. Folks need to have some understanding of how their giving benefits God's people beyond the walls of your church. If your congregation contributes to the wider church, as congregations do in the United Church of Christ, take a few minutes to explain how their church dollars are making a difference within the denomination.

Why not add a few minutes to recap the Sunday school lesson for that Sunday? This can be a way to generate interest in Sunday school and provide an opportunity for youth participation in the service.

A pastor once shared that her congregation was concerned about the noise that paper worship bulletins make in the increasingly shaky hands of her parishioners. To remedy the concern, she now prints the bulletin on cardstock because the heavier grade of paper is less noisy. The bulletin actually looks like an extra-large bookmark and allows for a bigger print font to make it easier to read.

Add a service to the week. Some churches offer an evening service, usually on Saturday or Sunday, but any day can work. The evening service is another opportunity for people to worship, especially for those who are not able to make a Sunday morning service. Or add a service on Sunday in addition to the regularly scheduled one. Some people—especially soccer moms and dads—prefer an early morning service so the rest of the day is free for other obligations.

Change the order of the service. Look at your current order of worship. If the offering always comes after the sermon, try moving it to a different place in the order of worship. If persons start leaving the sanctuary right after the benediction, invite them to stay and listen to a postlude. It is good to periodically assess the order of worship to see what's working and what might need changing. When I came to my church nine years ago, the order of worship had not changed significantly in more than forty years. How did I know this? Easy. My church kept a hard copy of virtually every worship bulletin for almost sixty years so I could see any changes that had taken place by looking in the bulletin archive. When you have a situation where something has not changed for that long, there is usually little need for assessment of its current effectiveness. Just look at how the world has changed since that order of worship was put in place. When the church first started using that order of worship, there was virtually no television, cable or otherwise. There were no computers, no cell phones, no 8-tracks, cassettes, CDs, or Blu-ray. There was no unleaded gas, no civil rights bill, no Voting Rights Act, and no school bus law. There were no projection screens, praise teams, or dance ministries. I'm sure you get my point. The world around the church had changed drastically, but the church was still clinging to the past. Let the past go, immerse yourself in the present, and embrace the future. Change is your friend, not your enemy.

The possibilities are endless. Use your imagination, consult with others, and dare to try something out of the ordinary.

Shorten Your Worship Service

If you look out on your congregation and find people glancing at their watches, your service may be too long. People who are truly engaged in worship don't worry about the time; those who are bored can't seem to stop checking the time.

As you look at your order of worship, note those things that take longer than others. Are there areas where the timing can be tightened? I visited a church in New England a while back; I was invited to preach, and I was looking forward to spending time with this congregation. I was surprised that the Passing of the Peace took over twenty minutes! The sanctuary was a mass of chaotic hugs and greetings that went on and on and on. The musicians played several songs before the pastor called the congregation back to order. Then, the announcements also took nearly twenty minutes; the speaker read a long list of those who were sick and shut in. While it was good to hear each name called, it lengthened the worship service considerably. In addition, the children's sermon was at least fifteen minutes long. The liturgical dance performance added another ten minutes to the service. The worship service started at 11:00 a.m., and I didn't get up to preach until nearly 1:00 p.m.! None of the members seemed put off by this, but I was worn out before I started to preach.

In this age of video games and television sound-bites, people's attention spans have shortened. Sitting for long periods of time can take a toll. Make sure that every phase of worship contributes to an environment where people expect God to show up. Anything that distracts from that should be eliminated from the service. An appropriate time and place should be created for those things that need to be done but may be more suitable in another setting. There is no reason to keep worshippers in church when worship is clearly over. Often so much time is wasted doing nonworship things that the worship experience becomes more like the meeting of a social club, fraternity, or political action committee. Never lose sight of the why of worship. We come to church as a gathered body of believers to give glory to our Creator, to give thanks to the son whom God sent to save the world, and to experience the power of the Holy Spirit— the presence of God in us and with us right now. It doesn't take all day to do that, as long as it is done in Spirit and in truth.

11

Lengthen Your Worship Service

At the other extreme are services that are what I call "no frills" services. There is minimal singing, a prayer, a Scripture, a sermon, and an offering—no more, no less! If this describes your worship service, consider lengthening it. Create a space where people can center themselves and focus on God. This may mean adding more time to the service. Pay attention to how people talk about the service; you can learn a lot as people exit the church after worship. Some folks hunger for more singing, more music, and more prayer. I have heard this point expressed many times, and I am always responsive to these kinds of comments from worshippers. When I first began preaching, one of the comments I would get at the door was, "Rev. Paul, I enjoyed that message, but we'd like to hear more of you." Eventually I realized that my sermons were too short!

My average message was about twelve minutes. I was not taking the time to develop the text and to include illustrations that may have helped worshippers understand the message and hear it more clearly. I took this suggestion to heart and began to practice preaching a more fulsome sermon designed to adequately feed the flock without them leaving bloated.

Another problem that I have noticed in churches that have become enslaved to the clock is singing congregational hymns too fast. Listen to the choir and the congregation as they sing. If they are not all together on the phrasing of a familiar song or hymn, then you are probably singing it too fast. The message of a hymn or praise song is what is truly important. If worshippers can't get the words out, then they won't get the message. Take the necessary time to sing songs so that people can understand the message the song is trying to convey.

In smaller churches, you can take the time to invite members to share their joys and concerns. This form of testimony can be a real bonding time for the congregation. People will share what is on their hearts and minds in an atmosphere of trust, knowing that other members are rejoicing or weeping with them over the matters of their lives. This practice often takes the form of the old testimony services common to many African American churches in years past. I've witnessed the power of testimony in many congregations; people feel that they are safe and are able to leave their burdens on the altar. Most important, whenever there is testimony in worship there is always someone there who needs to hear it and who will be blessed by what is shared. Do not underestimate the value of testimony no matter what size your congregation may be.

You may want to add more music to the service. Congregational singing is a great way to involve all the folks gathered for worship. This also allows for a wider range of music. If you have a number of musicians in the congregation, invite them to join the ministry of music and share their gifts. Instrumental musical interludes can be both powerful and inspiring in worship. If you have young musicians, this is an excellent way to involve them in the worship experience. Give them the opportunity to play during worship. The worshippers will love it, and the young people will be encouraged. Countless professional singers and musicians report that they got their start in the church.

You can add a number of elements to lengthen the service, but make sure that whatever you add brings depth and meaning to the experience. Don't try to fill up the time with things that are not relevant or meaningful. People know when you are just passing time. What you want to do is add to the ambience so that people are open to the movement of the Holy Spirit. People always respond to substance and don't check their watches when they are engaged.

A poorly planned and poorly executed worship service can never be short enough, and a meaningful and Spirit-filled one can never be too long!

Develop an Expectation
of Spontaneity

Christian churches through the ages have utilized scripted liturgy and carefully planned orders of worship. This style has served the church well for centuries. However, the danger exists that this style becomes an end unto itself and feels mechanical and detached. More emphasis is placed on following the order than waiting for the Holy Spirit to move. Any deviation from the accustomed order is seen as disrespectful and chaotic.

Throughout the Hebrew Bible (Old Testament), we find God admonishing Israel to make its worship and praise authentic, not rote and routine. The people had fallen into the routine of just doing things because they had always done them; they had forgotten the whys of worship. God wants worship to be the joyous expression of connection to God and others. There needs to be a sense of freedom in worship—freedom to express oneself in ways that move beyond the written liturgy and order of worship. The congregation should expect that something wonderful is about to happen every time God's people gather. We should live as if we are on the verge of a miracle, because we are!

One Sunday at church, a man came forward and said that he believed in Jesus and he wanted to be baptized. Immediately I began to think about the regularly scheduled baptismal service, when this could take place. I asked that he see me after the service, which he did. I found out that he would be leaving the city in two weeks and thus there would be no time to attend new member classes or wait for the scheduled baptism service. I received word that the man would be in service the following Sunday, so I decided to baptize him then without fanfare or announcement. I made up my mind that I would do this, but I told no one. That's what spontaneity is about. One Sunday early in the service I felt the Lord speaking to me clearly things that I needed to share with the congregation, so we exited the printed order of worship and I began to exhort to the people of God what God was giving me in that moment.

God has a number of ways of showing up. Sometimes it will be in song and music; sometimes in the heartfelt prayer of someone who understands what God can do; sometimes in the sincere stumbling of youth presenting a story; sometimes in the preached word; sometimes in the hug of the person sitting next to you in worship. We should enter worship expecting something out of the ordinary to happen. We never know how and in what form God will show up for us, so we need to develop a sense of wonder and anticipation. In the book of Acts, we find God showing up way beyond the box the people had drawn around God:

When the day of Pentecost had come, they were all together in one place. And suddenly from heaven there came a sound like the rush of a violent wind, and it filled the entire house where they were sitting. Divided tongues, as of fire, appeared among them, and a tongue rested on each of them. All of them were filled with the Holy Spirit and began to speak in other languages, as the Spirit gave them ability. —Acts 2:1–4 NRSV

Make Worship Interactive

One of the best ways to ignite worship is to create a space where people feel free to participate. Here, too, music can play an important role. Congregational singing is one option. Inviting members to bring musical instruments to worship is another. Members can join in by using their tambourines and maracas. Of course, music that is lively will invite hand clapping, toe tapping, and body swaying. Remember, though, that folks are not being entertained but rather are invited to participate fully in the worship experience.

Another option is to have the congregation read the Scripture in unison or responsively rather than have one person at the pulpit do it. The first time I witnessed this, I was impressed that the members gathered fully participated. The worship leader approached the microphone and announced the text. She asked that when the congregation had found the place in their Bibles to say "Amen!" When enough people said the magic word, she invited those who were able and willing to stand so they could recite the text together. She gave a short commentary on the text and started the recitation. The entire congregation responded; when they sat down, they were ready for the preached word. In some churches, the congregation stands for the reading of the Gospel text. Providing a bit of background helps. Don't preach the sermon, but give people some clues that will help them hear the text. Let them know that their participation is wanted and valued.

Worship services can include responsive readings—from the psalms, another text of the Bible, a poem, lyrics to a hymn or song, or a nonbiblical text. It can be energizing to mix it up a bit. Some Sundays, have a leader read and the members respond; sometimes, the reading can be divided between women and men, elders and youth, one side of the congregation and then the other. Be creative in deciding how the responsive reading will proceed.

I decided that on a given Sunday I wanted to engage the congregation in movement. I told the worshippers several weeks in advance that we would do this, but did not share exactly how. The day arrived. I had prepared a gospel line dance that I called the Jesus Shuffle—a takeoff of the popular Cupid Shuffle. (If you want to see it, it's on YouTube under Mt. Zion Congregational Church Cupid Shuffle.) When the Sunday came, to my surprise everyone in the church got up and engaged in the Jesus Shuffle. It was a great hit and is equally popular on YouTube.

Some congregations recite their denominational creed each Sunday. I've visited churches that include the statement of faith in the Sunday worship bulletin or on the inside cover of the main hymnal. By reciting the creed or statement together, members are reminded of their purpose and history and are connected to others in the tradition who profess the same convictions.

The point is that persons are active participants in worship. They are not passive observers waiting to be entertained. They should bring their whole lives to the worship experience. Worship is energized and enhanced when those gathered participate.

Ask People to Talk to One Another

Many churches now make time for worshippers to pass the peace or share in what is called a ritual of fellowship or friendship. They greet one another warmly and offer each other a blessing, which can be intimidating for the introverts in your midst. But once folks do this a few times, they get into the spirit of it. You might be surprised how many times people come to worship and no one says a word to them—the whole time they are in the church building. They can feel ignored and invisible. Certainly such actions do not embody extravagant welcome and hospitality.

I once witnessed the Reverend Dr. James Forbes, former pastor of the famous Riverside Church in New York City, get an entire auditorium of people up on their feet and sharing with each other. He asked a question, "When did you first meet God?" and invited folks to share in small clusters. It took a few minutes for the conversations to start because people were not accustomed to sharing their faith and were not expecting this to happen in a massive worship service. But before long, the auditorium of several hundred people was thundering with laughter and tears and hugs. By asking folks to talk to each other, Dr. Forbes had set the tone for people to do some authentic sharing, despite the fact that most of them did not know each other beforehand. It was a powerful moment, and I marveled at Dr. Forbes's capacity to take a risk. As I have tried this in various settings, it has worked every time. Something about the people of God talking to each other clears a space for the Holy Spirit to move and work.

I've seen some pastors ask the congregation to turn to their neighbors and repeat some words or phrases. During the sermon, in order to emphasize a point, the pastor may say, "Turn to your neighbor and say, 'God is able!'" You have to feel comfortable in making a request that people talk to each other, but it will ignite your worship and lend an air of spontaneity. The challenge may be containing the conversations, but what a good challenge to face!

Add Drama to Worship

The Bible is filled with drama, so it's not a stretch to say that our worship services can be more dramatic than they are. In fact, worship can be seen as re-creating the drama of salvation history. Think about ways to dramatize the Scripture as well as the biblical story that will be preached.

A friend who was pastor of a small storefront church in Chicago related the story of a Good Friday service at the church. A huge wooden cross hung on the wall of the large room that served as sanctuary and dining hall for feeding the hungry and homeless. On Good Friday, the liturgy consisted of Scripture readings and congregational singing. Between each of the Seven Last Words, members were invited to hammer a large nail into the cross to symbolically act out the crucifixion drama. As each person approached the cross, there was a noticeable change in body language. The pastor said the ringing of the hammer against the nail was a dramatic way of bringing home the horror of the crucifixion for modern folks who don't really think about the pain and suffering Jesus experienced that day. The nails remained in the cross until sunrise service on Sunday when the congregation returned from a lakeside service to have breakfast together at the church. Then they celebrated God's resurrection of Jesus, but they lived with the uncertainty of Good Friday until Sunday. This is a creative way to bring the biblical story to life so that everyone could find themselves in the story.

Each year in our church on Maundy Thursday, at the end of the service I select a symbol of suffering for each member to experience. Since we share this service in the fellowship hall of the church around tables, it is easy to place the symbols on each table. One year I decided to go in a different direction. I wanted Jesus to carry the cross through the fellowship hall as the symbol of suffering. I had one of the young adults dress in an appropriate costume, placed a crown of thorns (real thorns) on his head, and had our custodian build an eight-foot cross for him to carry on his back. We dimmed the lights and sang the spiritual "Were You There When They Crucified My Lord" as he carried the heavy cross through the room. Halfway across the room he intentionally stumbled and fell, then struggled to rise and continued to make his way through the room. The sobs in the room were loud and palpable. This simple act of drama helped the worshippers experience the suffering of Jesus in a very real way. On Easter, Jesus entered the church with a throng of children shouting his name. Again, worshippers were visibly moved.

In a recent conversation, a pastor talked about worshipping on Pentecost Sunday. The worship team decided that when the text talked about the Holy Spirit coming down as tongues of fire, they would release red rose petals from the sanctuary rafters to fall gently on the worshippers. What a marvelous way of bringing the text to life.

The most dramatic worship I experienced was at the Apostolic Church of God in Chicago where the late Bishop Arthur

M. Brazier was pastor. The church building is a modern facility that can accommodate a full orchestra in the chancel area.
One Sunday, Bishop Brazier approached the pulpit and began
reading Psalm 150:1–6. The lights in the sanctuary were dim,
almost off, except for the small light on the pulpit from where
the bishop read. He read slowly and with dramatic pauses and
flair:

> Praise the [HOLY ONE]!
>
> Praise God in [the] sanctuary;
>   praise [God] in [God's] mighty firmament!
> Praise [God] for [God's] mighty deeds;
>   praise [God] according to [God's] surpassing greatness!
>
> Praise [God] with trumpet sound;
>   praise [God] with lute and harp!
> Praise [God] with tambourine and dance;
>   Praise [God] with strings and pipe!
> Praise [God] with clanging cymbals;
>   praise [God] with loud clashing cymbals!
> Let everything that breathes praise the LORD!
>   Praise the Lord!

He paused after each verse, and we could hear the rising tones
of trumpets, lutes, harps, tambourines, strings, pipes, cymbals—each additional instrument adding to the volume of the
sound—and as each instrument joined the musical chorus, the
lights grew brighter and brighter. As the lights got brighter, we
saw the orchestra seeming to rise from the floor of the chancel;
we couldn't believe our eyes. With each verse of the Scripture,
the lights went higher and the sound became louder.

When the bishop read the last verse of the psalm, the sanctuary was filled with light and the sounds of the orchestral instruments. Needless to say, the worshippers were soon on their feet praising God with their hallelujahs and amens! I was profoundly moved by the drama, and I still get chills thinking about the worship moment. I had not witnessed such drama in worship before and was moved beyond words. The orchestra played a traditional hymn and Bishop Brazier sat down. He didn't utter another word until he pronounced the benediction. In the meantime, the congregation continued praising God accompanied by the orchestra for at least twenty minutes. What a worship experience, with lights, sounds, and scripture!

There are so many instances in the Bible where we can add drama and bring the texts to life. Gather the artists in your congregation to see what is possible in your context. I know that there are actors waiting to offer the gifts to God. They only need to be asked.

Add Dance to Worship

Liturgical dance is a growing phenomenon in congregations regardless of denomination. Dancing as part of worship, however, is nothing new. Miriam led women and men in dancing and singing after the Hebrew people crossed the Red Sea from oppression in Egypt (Exodus 15:20–21). Even King David was known to step lightly to honor God (2 Samuel 6:12–15). Just as David danced before God, we too can dance in celebration of what God has done for us and in anticipation of what God will do on our behalf. Dancing is not sacrilegious but rather is a gift of movement to praise God. As a person who studied dance and has been dancing for over thirty years, I am always blessed to see dance done well in worship. Our church, unlike many, has a more than forty year history of liturgical dance. Through the years I have been blessed to work with and learn from some awesome liturgical dancer/choreographers, including Jewel MacLauren of Chicago and Edna Duffy of Cleveland, Ohio. These liturgical dance pioneers committed their lives to bringing the medium of dance to the house of worship, with tremendous results.

Some years ago, my wife and I visited an Episcopal church in Washington, D.C., for a liturgical dance performance. We were greatly surprised to see that the church had removed all of the pews and created a circle of folding chairs in the sanctuary to facilitate dance. What an awesome commitment to dance in worship!

In meaningful and powerful ways, liturgical dance is embodied prayer. Dancers offer their gifts to a variety of music—contemporary Christian music, recorded music, traditional hymns. It is an opportunity to be creative. Hardly anyone can watch dancers in worship and not be moved. Liturgical dance is inspiring and moving. Choreographed and sincere body movements, with or without streamers or banners, draw us in and we are touched to the core. Liturgical dance is not a spectator sport. It is an authentic offering of the body in praise of God.

17

Add Poetry to Worship

Fred B. Craddock, retired preaching professor, has been a strong advocate of using poetry in worship. I saw a video he did some years ago where he lifted up an example. In the film *Camelot*, Robert Goulet sings, "If Ever I Would Leave You." He offers a litany trying to figure out the best time to leave his beloved—not in summer, not in autumn, not in winter, not in spring—each season has its own beauty that would make parting too painful to bear. Craddock has jokingly said it would have been easier for Goulet to just say he wouldn't leave his beloved. But the words, the images, the emotions evoked— that's the power of poetry.

A poem can say so much more than prose; it's no wonder that large portions of our Bible, especially the psalms and the prophetic books, are poems. They capture images that come alive and breathe.

A friend said that her seminary preaching professor told the class that every preacher should have a favorite poet. They should learn everything they can about that poet's life—the joys, the tragedies, the disappointments, the triumphs. Then the preacher can connect the poetry's story with the biblical stories and offer fresh images and insights to the congregation.

Many lyrics to rap and hip-hop are poems with a beat. If you have young people in your congregation, seek their help in identifying spiritually grounded lyrics to add to the worship service. A number of very fine hip-hop musicians have a spiritual and positive message. Set aside a month when you can have a different poet in the church to read or recite a poem appropriate to the theme of worship that day. People will become engaged and excited about this seemingly new worship form. You will be amazed at the number of poets and readers that you have in your congregation. Good poetry, in its various forms, will enhance and ignite your worship.

Add Pageantry to Worship

A way to ignite worship is to add the drama of pageantry to your service. This can be easily done during the processional of the choir, worship leaders, and ministers. Choose music that is lively and up-tempo, or select powerful classical music that can be played from a recording. Many fanfares and processionals are easily adapted. Have the youth, liturgical dancers or members of the congregation enter the worship space waving banners, flags, ribbons, streamers, or cultural symbols. As they dance down the aisle, invite the congregation to add to the pageantry by waving streamers that have been distributed or by playing hand instruments such as tambourines or gourds. The processional could include drums.

This kind of pageantry also works well as a recessional. The point is to express freedom, joy, love, and gratitude. Pageantry can set a tone for worship that is Spirit-led and Spirit-filled. The movements should be choreographed, but remember this is not a performance. It is an expression of joy that sets the tone for an enhanced and enriched worship experience as the people celebrate being in the presence of God.

I attended the anniversary service of a local church where the young people used pageantry to help the congregation remember and renew their baptismal vows. They came down the aisle dressed in white robes at a certain point in the service and lightly sprinkled the entire congregation with water using large palm branches. This was most effective and helped us all to remember the importance of baptism.

Involve People of All Ages in Worship

Worship is not just for adults of a certain age. Worship is an opportunity for all God's people, regardless of age, to anticipate and wait for the presence of God, and this includes children.

For various reasons, congregations have developed patterns that make some feel like second-class members in the church. The children are pushed aside in classrooms so that they do not disrupt the service. True, all that happens in worship does not hold the interest of young children. Still, they should feel welcomed and included in the service.

Including a Children's Moment before sending the children to Sunday school or other activity is one way to welcome them into the service.

Some churches have Youth Sunday services specifically for the young people in the congregation; often, these are fifth Sundays of the year. Since there are not too many of those, I suggest that Youth Sundays become a regular part of the service rotation.

In addition to specific Sundays for youth and young adults, they should be included in every phase of church life. There should be youth on the church boards—on the church council, on the usher board, and on the deacon board. I have seen this done effectively in many churches, in which youth participate in almost every Sunday service, reading Scripture, leading prayer, lifting the offering. They feel an ownership and investment in worship. They participate willingly, and their capacity for leadership is enhanced.

Likewise, the elders of the church should be included. Sometimes, the elderly in our congregation can feel like they have outlived their usefulness and their gifts are not sought. But they bring wisdom and experience to the worship time. They should be invited to be active worship leaders. Some do not want to impose, so a specific invitation would be welcomed. Having young and old work together creates a beautiful portrait for visitors and members alike to see each time the church gathers to worship.

Explore Cultural Diversity in Worship

God loves diversity! Even a cursory glance at creation bears this out. How else can we explain aardvarks and butterflies, elephants and ants, roses and dandelions? Diversity is a gift, and vital worship is infused with elements of cultural diversity. By bringing into worship elements that recognize the diversity of God's creation, we honor God and embrace all as sisters and brothers. Your church may not be as racially and ethnically diverse as you would want. Still, resources are available to help you set a tone of openness to the gifts of sisters and brothers who are different from you.

Almost all denominations now have culturally diverse and culturally sensitive hymnals, prayer books, and worship aids. Cultivate an openness to ethnic music—African, African American, Hispanic/Latino/a, Japanese, Dutch, French, Caribbean, British, Irish, and so on. The point is not to exploit or misuse elements of cultural importance but rather to celebrate the gifts of diversity among God's people. In some settings, cultural diversity is celebrated in food, music, and dress. Much is to be learned, however, by delving deeper into cultures that differ from our own. It's one thing for the choir to sing "Swing Low, Sweet Chariot" and appreciate its melodic and soothing rhythms. It's another thing altogether to hear the story behind the spiritual—how the song was used in the invisible church of the slaves, expressing both hope in a future where freedom reigned and as a signal for the Underground Railroad where slaves escaped oppression and fled toward freedom.

Whatever elements you choose to include in your worship service, be sure to share with the congregation the meaning behind those elements and how they enrich your lives—not because they are exotic, cute, lively, or colorful. But rather because they are the expressions of one part of the body of Christ that enhances us all.

A dear friend of mine once served a multicultural church as co-pastor in a major city. The church consisted of an English-speaking congregation and a Spanish-speaking congregation, each with a pastor. The two congregations held separate services except for Communion, Christmas, Easter, and a few other occasions. During the once-monthly bilingual Communion service, the co-pastors established the tradition of translating every word spoken or sung into English and Spanish.

One day, my friend, whose first language is English, suggested that they leave some portions of the service in the native language of the speaker. So they tried it. My friend explained to the congregation (and this was translated) that she trusted her sisters and brothers to pray for her in Spanish; she didn't need to know what was said. The congregation affirmed this, and the two congregations began to do more things together because a sense of community and trust developed.

If there is adequate cultural diversity within your congregation, you might want to establish a diversity ministry to celebrate the richness of the many heritages that make up your worshipping congregation. We have done this in our church with great success. Our diversity ministry not only celebrates racial and ethnic diversity but also the diversity of sexual orientations that make up the tapestry of our church and denomination. This can be a rich resource for growth and learning for your church and an opportunity to ignite your worship with the diversity of the human family.

Develop a Worship Team and Meet with Them Frequently

Your worship team should be made up of those who are responsible for various areas of worship within the church. It should include the pastor(s) choir director, musician(s), worship leader, sound or audiovisual person, and other persons whom you may add depending on the size and setting of your church. The purpose of the worship team is to facilitate the improvement of the atmosphere for worship in your church. The team should come together regularly to discuss and evaluate the context of worship. This is the time for visioning, innovation, and change to come forth. All members of the team should know that their ideas and thoughts are valued and can help ignite the worship life of the congregation. Set regular dates and time limits for the team meetings; it is very easy in the hectic atmosphere of doing God's work in the church to lose sight of the importance of taking time for reflection and evaluation of the ministry of worship.

You may also wish to invite a member of the congregation not specifically involved in worship planning or implementation to be involved with the team to help share the perspective of those in the pews. At times it is hard to be objective about something that you are intimately involved in. The "perspective of the pew" helps the team to understand how the majority of the congregation experiences worship and thus brings a fresh important and much-needed dimension to the team.

The newly formed worship team may want to begin their ministry with a retreat: a time set apart for worship, singing, prayer, sharing, community building, and brainstorming ideas for worship facilitation. This can be all day, two days, a weekend— whatever works for your group. Have available for the retreat an outline of the church year—religious seasons (Advent, Lent, Easter, Pentecost), national observances (Martin L. King Jr. Day, Memorial Day, Labor Day, Mother's Day, Father's Day), cultural observances (Kwanzaa, Chinese New Year, Cinco de Mayo), congregational observances (Homecoming Sunday, Church and Pastor's Anniversaries, Graduates Sunday, Usher Board Sunday)—those times of special celebration. If you preach from the lectionary, bring a list of the texts for each Sunday. This is a time for the worship team to vision and dream about worship for your church. Make this a fun yet deeply spiritual time. There are games and activities that can help people remember Bible stories, think about what the sanctuary should look like each Sunday and consider themes for the Sunday worship times.

After the retreat, determine how often the team will meet. Some worship teams meet monthly, working several months out. Others meet quarterly to check in and evaluate how things are going. Do whatever works best for your group and church. The team will be invested in worship and will help others get excited about worship times. New energy will emerge as people really begin to see how exciting, powerful, and meaningful worship can be.

Establish a Standard of Excellence in All

In all that we do, we should strive to bring our very best. Our God deserves the best of our gifts, and we fall short by not holding to a standard of excellence. This does not mean we are not allowed to make mistakes, but when we make mistakes, let it be because of anxiety and not because we have not prepared. I have always said that everyone's standard of excellence is not the same. Dr. Lawrence Neale Jones, while dean of Howard University School of Divinity, used to share this story to illustrate this point for his students. "Once I had a man build some kitchen cabinets for our home. He worked long and hard on the job, and when he had finished he called me into the kitchen and proudly presented to me his finished product, 'Aren't they nice, Dean?' he asked. 'Nice' is not the word that I would have chosen. To my surprise and dismay the cabinets were clearly hanging crooked on the wall, but in the carpenter's mind he had done a 'nice' job." Everyone's concept of excellence is not the same.

It is important that you set the standard of excellence in your church and maintain it. Others will see that standard and rise to it. I heard Dr. Howard Thurman say once that "God places a crown above our heads that we spend our lives trying to rise up to."

All who lead worship should rehearse and prepare their role before Sunday worship. That means reading the Scripture ahead of time in order to be familiar with it, asking help to pronounce difficult words. That means thinking about the prayers before Sunday—not that it has to be scripted, but some thought should have been given ahead of time so that the remarks are thoughtful, inclusive, and not rambling or incoherent; it means choosing and rehearsing music that supports the entire worship experience. Worship is not always perfect; because we are human, we stumble and misstep. But the "mistakes" should never stem from a lack of preparation. We do our best to be ready and turn the service over to the Holy Spirit. We offer the best of who we are and what we do before our God—Creator, Redeemer, and Sustainer.

Part Three

MUSIC

Music is universal. It speaks to our souls,
evoking emotions and memories that can transform
not only our worship but also our lives,
individually and communally.
Let music set the tone and pace
for your worship.

Upgrade Your Sound System

Whatever you plan to do to enhance your music program, make sure you have a sound system that accommodates your needs. A good sound system is a solid investment in igniting your worship. You will notice a marked difference in the quality of the music and spoken word when you install a quality sound system. Many churches were built for pipe organs and vocalists. The acoustics of a sanctuary may work against you as you revamp your worship service.

Work with a sound engineer to determine what adjustments you may need to make in order for your music ministry to thrive. Some solutions are simple: adding cushions to wooden pews, suspending microphones from the ceiling, carpeting parts of the floor, adding Plexiglas panels around the drums. Other solutions may require long-term investments in architectural or structural changes—rewiring the sanctuary, constructing or deconstructing walls, moving the choir loft. Be sure to do your homework before suggesting any changes to make sure you are exercising good stewardship of your funds.

When you add a new sound system, take the time and make the investment to train those who will operate it. There is nothing worse than to have a gift that you do not use or use improperly. Training is not hard to find. Most installers are happy to train whoever will be operating the sound system. I always encourage pastors to get the training as well. If your A/V person is ill on any given Sunday, you need to be able to at least turn on the system and set the levels. Good sound is a necessity for a vital worship experience.

Add Drums

I remember hearing a pastor relate a story. He was invited to preach at a tall-steepled church. He was prepared for a sedate service with a printed worship bulletin with the standard elements: gathering, singing, prayer, preaching, offering, and benediction. He expected a chancel choir singing some of the standards of Christendom to the resounding waves from a massive pipe organ.

He expected the service to move along but with little energy or excitement. It was going to be a "nice" service, and he was fine with that. His custom was to arrive early at the church so he could check out the arrangement of the sanctuary. As the pastor escorted him into the sanctuary, he was surprised to see a set of drums next to a piano. He asked if the drums were ever used in worship. The pastor enthusiastically replied yes! So instead of a staid, stuffy service, the preacher found himself clapping to the beat of the drums—played by a young woman of the congregation!

I am often asked what young people connect with most musically in the twenty-first century. My answer is always the same. Bass and beat. The sound of the bass and the beat of the drum are key elements in contemporary music, and for many in the Echo Boomer generation (those born between 1982 and 1995), these elements are what help them feel connected to the music of the church. In fact, for many in the previous generation the same is true. Those who grew up listening to Motown and rock and roll are going to be hard pressed to find a point of connection in a worship service where only a pipe organ is utilized. If you want to ignite your worship service, you must be open to all forms of musical expression. Drums are a key element.

There is a large Catholic church in my neighborhood, and I watch in amazement as the people rush to worship as I pass by both on Saturday evening and for several services on Sunday. I wondered what was going on in this church that was attracting so many worshippers, while in the same city other Catholic churches were closing by the score. I found out one day when I was invited to a neighbor's wedding at the church. Immediately upon entering the sanctuary my eyes were drawn to the drum set near the organ and the keyboard next to them, but there was much more. There were tympani and African drums, and during the wedding the priest played the guitar and sang to the couple. Here was the answer to the puzzle: this church had found a way to bridge the gap between its musical past and its present and was positioning itself to claim the future. There were clearly no limits on what this vibrant church could or would do to worship God and reach the people with the message of the gospel.

We might associate drums with more contemporary worship services. But drums can be used in almost any setting. They add drama to worship. The skills of the drummer set the pace and tone for enlivened worship. Everyone, regardless of age, circumstance, background, or condition, can relate to the drum. If you ever watch babies and toddlers when drums are playing, they instinctively begin moving to the beat. The steady beat of the drums calls to each of us in ways that are inspiring and healing.

Consult with a trained musician to determine the acoustics of your worship space. You want people to feel the rhythm but not leave with a pounding headache.

If no drummers emerge from your congregation, look to your local high school or college for folks willing to play during worship services. You should not have a problem finding a drummer, if you are determined to include this important instrumentation in your revitalized worship experience.

Add Horns

Almost any horn is suitable for use in worship. Typically, horns are divided into brass horns (trumpets, trombones, etc.), and woodwinds (clarinets, flutes, oboes). The distinction is based on the sound of the instrument, not the material from which it is made. At various times, many churches include flutes, saxophones, trumpets, and French horns in special services of worship. These instruments, because they are unexpected in worship, help people to feel their way into authentic worship. To ignite your worship, consider using these instruments on a fairly regular basis. The congregation will be surprised, and pleased, at the harmonies and melodies that horns add to a worship service.

In our church we frequently have jazz services where a saxophone player is used. This brings a level of authenticity to what I call our Service of Sacred Jazz. The Reverend Dr. Dwight Andrews, pastor of First Congregational Church in Atlanta, is renowned for the jazz services that he orchestrates in his church and commonly experiences standing-room-only crowds for these creative worship experiences.

The Reverend Dr. Ozzie E. Smith Jr., pastor of Covenant United Church of Christ in South Holland, Illinois, just outside of Chicago, is another musical pioneer in the use of horns in worship. Rev. Ozzie is a trained musician who has had opportunities to play with some of the most outstanding vocalists of our day. These could have led to lucrative jobs that were international in scope. Rev. Ozzie, however, decided to dedicate his musical gift to the glory of God, and what a blessing he has been to the church. Rev. Ozzie plays the saxophone and several other instruments as well, and he employs a variety of different types of music. He plays more traditional hymns in addition to contemporary sacred music. He uses his saxophone to enhance and supplement his preaching—in some instances, his playing *is* the sermon. The music moves people and evokes emotions and memories which assure listeners that they are connected to God in ways that words cannot convey. I've seen people cry openly because they are overwhelmed by their emotions, feeling the presence of God through the music. Rev. Ozzie is a gifted musician and preacher. He embodies what it means to ignite worship with sound and word.

The horns may be part of a larger music program at your church or be used for particular songs. Musical solos can go a long way in igniting and energizing worship. If you are not a musician, seek out those who are and invite them to join your worship services. Again, if no one emerges in your congregation, this is a great opportunity to seek out students at the high school or local college.

Add Strings and Guitars

The use of stringed instruments in worship is ancient. The Bible makes notice of various stringed instruments:

> Rejoice in the [Holy One], O you righteous.
>   Praise befits the upright.
> Praise the [Holy One] with the lyre;
>   make melody to [God] with the harp of ten strings.
> Sing a new song;
>   play skillfully on the strings, with loud shouts.
>   —Psalm 33:1–3 NRSV

> The [Sovereign One] will save me,
>   and we will sing to stringed instruments
>   all the days of our lives,
>   at the house of the [Sovereign One].
>   —Isaiah 38:20 NRSV

Stringed instruments include the violin, guitar, cello, harp, bass, and numerous others. Like horns, strings can greatly enhance worship by bringing unexpected harmonies and melodies. Do not limit the use of strings to contemporary services. All services and many kinds of music can be adapted to stringed instruments. You may want to consider using string solos for preludes and postludes, and as background music for prayers or special readings.

When we think of guitars in worship, our minds may drift back to the days of the 1960s and 1970s when such use was popular. Many campus ministries are remembered fondly because of congregational singing accompanied by guitars. Today, many summer camps worship includes guitar music. In fact, I know a youth minister who never travels without his guitar. When all else fails, bring out the guitar!

Although I am only half joking, I know a guitar can greatly enhance worship. Hardly anyone can protest against the melodic strumming of a guitar. Of course, there may be some resistance to electric guitars or bass guitars; we normally associate these instruments with rock bands and contemporary services.

We were blessed for many years at our church to have a former cellist from the Cleveland Orchestra as a member of our family. He would play frequently for worship and holiday musical programs. He freely shared his gift with the congregation, and all of us grew as a result of his musical generosity.

As with most of the instruments I have lifted up, all kinds of stringed instruments can ignite worship, and even traditional hymns can be adapted for use with electric guitars. Again, connect with a skilled musician who can help you determine what will work best for your congregation.

Add Keyboards

Many churches still rely on the pipe organ to set the musical stage for worship. Churches have spent many thousands of dollars refurbishing and tuning these time-honored instruments. Indeed, some church music sounds "right" only when played on the tried and true pipe organ. Some churches have even undergone intense and catastrophic fights over the pipe organ—some will remember how their parents or grandparents sacrificed to help pay for the organ. Stories galore emerge when you talk about adding instrumentation beyond the pipe organ.

Let me establish this up front: I love the music of the pipe organ, and I feel that its use can add exponentially to worship when it is played by a skilled and anointed musician. There is no rival to the majestic and stately sounds that come out of this, the largest instrument ever built. I was blessed to grow up in Philadelphia where the largest playable pipe organ in the world can be found. The John Wanamaker Organ, in the Grand Court of Macy's department store in downtown Philadelphia, is a must-hear for any organist or church musician. My parents would take us there for the daily concerts whenever we were downtown shopping. I grew up in an Episcopal church with a pipe organ and a gifted organist, so my appreciation for the organ was nurtured from my childhood. This has always been a blessing to me but not so for the organists who have served with me in ministry. My expectation of an organist has been shaped by my experiences and exposure, and thus I know that a poor or lazy organist produces poor organ music and the results are devastating for a church wishing to ignite its worship.

The addition of keyboards provides a modern, fresh, and lively sound to your worship. Keyboards appeal to the younger members of your congregation as well as the young at heart. A digital keyboard gives you the opportunity to bring in instruments that you could not afford to pay for. They open up new vistas of worship music for a congregation. Any congregation seeking to ignite worship should consider the enormous benefit that the use of keyboards can bring.

Add Hand Instruments
That the Congregation Can Play

Non-musicians can play any number of small hand instruments to add rhythms and a lively beat to the music used for the worship service. Many of them are fairly inexpensive, and members may even have them at their homes. Hand instruments can include bells, cow bells, maracas, tambourines, cymbals, hand/ finger cymbals, chimes, rattles, gourds, sticks, rainmaker sticks, castanets, cabasas, triangles, kazoos, whistles, drums, congas, bongos, and shakers. These hand instruments are easy to master and allow worshippers of all ages to participate.

Hand instruments add color to the worship music. Don't worry if these varied instruments sound chaotic. The point is to add some fun to worship. And the Bible encourages us to make a joyful noise unto our God!

We have a member in our church who plays the tambourine. She takes this musical gift quite seriously, and when she plays it adds to the rhythm, fun, and spontaneity of the worship experience. I have also experienced worship services where members brought other hand instruments such as maracas and cabasas (a large gourd). Having these instruments in worship added a life and energy to worship that took away the feeling of performance from the worship experience. In worship where the members are encouraged to bring their individual musical gifts to the experience, there is always vitality and energy.

Hire a New Minister/ Director of Music/Choir Director

Sometimes a change in music leader can be a good thing. A new minister of music, director of music, or choir director brings fresh ideas to worship. He or she will also bring expertise and experience to help the congregation think about worship in new ways. New leadership may also be reflective of changes in the congregation's demographics. If your congregation is drawing young couples with children, a different minister/director of music, or choir director may understand better the kinds of music that will support those gathered. If your congregation is drawing people from differing racial-ethnic backgrounds, a new leader of a different ethnicity may be just the ticket for folks to feel welcomed and comfortable.

Think about what kind of worship experience you want to foster as well as whom you would like to attract to your worship service. If you want a lively, upbeat worship, you may need to seek out someone who has a love for that kind of music and worship. If you want more cultural diversity in worship, you need to select someone who is culturally sensitive and has some knowledge about multicultural worship.

In some cases, the person who has been doing the job for years may be ready for a change themselves. Or a short hiatus might allow the current leader to retool or hone new skills for the ministry to which they have been called. Sometimes you just need a new person to bring about the change that will ignite worship.

Don't be afraid to explore the possibility of hiring someone new. The point is to find persons who understand the purpose of worship and are willing to work with the congregation to enliven the worship experience.

Start a Praise Team

Many progressive congregations now have included praise teams in their worship services. A praise team is usually a small group of singers, which should include soprano, alto, tenor, and bass, if possible. They will normally be accompanied by musicians that may include bass and electric guitarist, pianist, keyboard player, organist (usually Hammond), drummer, saxophonist, or others. In some settings, the praise team replaces the traditional choir; they set the tone by getting the congregation singing. There is no need for hymnals or song sheets because praise songs are easy to sing; there is enough repetition for all to join in. Often the music that the praise team sings is projected on a screen to further facilitate congregational singing.

Praise teams exude energy that is contagious, which helps the congregation engage in worship. These teams model the joy that should be a part of every worship service. The praise teams also show the congregation how to express themselves and to open themselves to the movement of the Holy Spirit. Selected music focuses on a theme, a biblical verse, an image, a word—the point is to help people move into a deeper relationship with God. The emphasis is on feeling, not as an artificial emotion but as an avenue into communion with God. The praise team sets the tone for worship and signals to the worshippers the level of formality for the service. Praise teams let worshippers know that we've gathered to have a good time praising God and they are invited to join in.

Start a Children's Choir

Children love to sing! Have you ever noticed that infants start to "sing" along as soon as they can make some sounds? Capitalize on this innocent eagerness to share and lift voices in song.

The choir director can bring the children together or seek someone in the congregation or community who is willing to take this on. This might also be an opportunity to invite a high school or college musician in the congregation or community to provide leadership. A children's choir requires parental support and some rehearsal times. Make sure there are regular times in worship when the children's choir can offer their ministry of song to the congregation. You can invest in robes or let the children sing in their Sunday clothes.

The songs selected should be fun and conducive to young voices. Congregations enjoy watching their children and grand-children involved in worship, and the kids have a great time, too!

I never knew how much our members enjoyed hearing and seeing the young people sing until I took time to do some listening sessions with the congregation. One of the most important desires of the congregation was to see the little children participate in worship. I learned an important lesson in the process. Children can be a great blessing as an exciting and vital part of the worship experience!

Start a Teen Choir

Like the children, teens need ways to be involved in worship. A teen choir is a great way to invite them to participate. The choir director or another person can take charge of the teen choir.

Teens need to have the opportunity to pray together, and they should have significant input into the kind of music they offer. This is an opportunity to have some different kind of music in worship. Don't be afraid to let the teens lift up hip-hop songs or spoken words that are spiritual and appropriate for Sunday worship, which also values the contribution of the teens in your congregation. Many teen choirs include persons who are friends of teens in the church; let all who are willing to show up for rehearsals and Sunday worship participate.

In one of my first ministries out of seminary I was responsible for youth ministry in a large congregation. One of my favorite parts of that ministry was the youth choir. The young people loved to get together for rehearsal and to sing in worship. The choir director, a young adult himself, was not afraid to allow the teens to express themselves in their own way, and thus the kids stayed engaged. The adult worshippers also got a kick out of seeing the young people be themselves in worship. A dear friend of mind puts it well: "We make a great mistake when we try to make children act like little adults." She is right! Youth and children must be able to experience and express God and their faith in their own language. This will not hinder the church. It will ignite it in vibrant worship!

33

Start a Community Choir

A good way to involve community members is to start a community choir. The choir can sing on special occasions, Homecoming Sunday, or Church Anniversary. Or you may want to incorporate the community choir more fully in the life of the congregation. You may want to have the community choir sing at neighborhood celebrations; you have the flexibility to create opportunities beyond the walls of your church.

You will be surprised at how many people in the area surrounding the church would like an opportunity to lift their voices in song with others. You won't know until you issue the invitation. Members may have friends who are looking for the chance to sing. Let them come and blend their voices with others.

One church convened a community choir and invited students from the local high school and college to participate. The only requirement was that students come to rehearsal before the worship service. Students didn't have to show up every week; they participated as they were able. They felt welcomed at the church and often made some sacrifice to participate. Many congregations have done this with great success. It is a great way to evangelize the community. Remember: Where children come, parents will follow.

There may be church members who used to sing in the choir but prefer not to have the rigors of weekly rehearsals. The community choir might be the perfect venue for them to share their gifts without making a heavy commitment.

Add More Congregational Singing

I know of few congregations where people complain that there is too much singing. Singing is a way for everyone to participate in the worship service. Singing unites people and sets the pace for worship. Singing connects people to God in powerful ways. It is also an opportunity to introduce new music into the worship repertoire. Congregational singing lets every worshipper know that he or she is valued as participant and that each one has a contribution to make to the worship service.

When introducing new songs, make sure there is ample rehearsal time so that everyone can sing with confidence. This may require the choir director and musicians to teach the song before worship so that members are familiar with it. New music allows the worship leaders to share information about the song and its meanings. Congregational singing is a social act that enhances worship immensely.

One Sunday I decided to teach the congregation to sing in four-part harmony, so I taught a simple song that I know well, and that they could easily learn. I was surprised at how everyone in the church felt free to participate and at the affirming comments I received about this new addition to worship. People love to sing, so don't limit their opportunities to worship God in song.

Start a Band or Orchestra

Again, music is key to igniting powerful and meaningful worship. In addition to current musicians, consider starting a band or orchestra to supplement the musical offerings during worship. This is a great opportunity to invite community members to join in worship, or you may have members in your congregation who are looking for opportunities to play sacred music.

A number of musicians in my congregation love being in worship. I dare not let them sit in the pews as if they have no gifts. So I invite them to participate in the worship services— they sing, play piano, drums—whatever their gifts are, we make a space for them. They bring such energy and depth to worship. A few times during the year, we feature them in special services. For instance, the Sunday after our annual revival, we hold a jazz vespers service that draws the congregation as well as community members who come to worship with us.

Again, this is chance to include high school and college students who are looking for a musical outlet. This is also a way to introduce different genres of music to the congregation. Music has the power to broaden our horizons and connect us to the Divine. So, let the music play!

Part Four

PREACHING

*Preaching is the proclamation of the Christian message
to the gathered faith community.
We are assured that whenever two or three are gathered,
Jesus is in the midst of us.
Each week, we gather to hear God's Word.
Preaching is a spiritual discipline that requires our best.
The preacher should strive to craft biblically based
and theologically sound sermons.
Remember that the sermon is not about you
but rather about the good news of what God has done,
is doing, and will do through the life, ministry, death,
and resurrection of Jesus Christ.*

Preach from the Lectionary

The lectionary is the weekly list of biblical passages to be read and heard in Christian worship services. For each week, the lectionary designates readings from the Hebrew Bible (Old Testament) and the Christian Scriptures (New Testament). Lectionary-based churches around the world hear the same Scripture on any given Sunday—regardless of denomination. The lectionary's purpose is to provide a way to preach, hear, and study major sections of the Bible in an orderly fashion.

The most widely used lectionary is the Revised Common Lectionary (RCL) used by both Catholics and Protestants. The schedule of readings include: a passage from the Hebrew Bible, the Apocrypha* (for Catholic circles), or the Acts of the Apostles; a passage from one of the psalms; another from either the book of Revelation or the Epistles; and finally a passage from one of the four Gospels. The schedule of readings is a three-year cycle: Year A focuses on Matthew; Year B focuses on Mark; Year C focuses on Luke. Only the Gospel of John lacks a year

---

*The Apocrypha (from the Greek meaning "hidden" or "concealed") are those books in the Catholic Bible not found in Jewish Bibles. They are often grouped together between the Old and New Testaments in Protestant Bibles. The focus of the apocryphal writings is the working out of God's purposes for creation and about the efforts to oppose God's plan. Jesus Christ is the climax of God's work for creation.

devoted to it. Parts of John are used at important points in the Christian year—Christmas, Lent, and Easter.

The lectionary helps Christians move through the church year, which begins with the first Sunday of Advent and moves through Christmas, Epiphany, Ash Wednesday, Lent, Palm Sunday, Maundy Thursday, Good Friday, Easter, Ascension Sunday, and Pentecost. The cycle then begins again. The lectionary is a tool to shape worship, allowing both preacher and laity to read and study the same passages. The use of the lectionary provides persons with a comprehensive understanding of the Bible and the church year.

The lectionary also provides the preacher with texts each week so that there is not a hunt to come up with texts on one's own. The lectionary also offers a wide range of Scripture and themes so that one's preferences do not dominate preaching. In the end, the aim of preaching is to bring a word of good news to God's people—a word that is accurate, fresh, informed, and interesting.

Renowned lectionary advocate and scholar Dr. Thomas E. Dipko told me many years ago that "each preacher has a lectionary whether it is the Revised Common Lectionary or not." To test this I reviewed the sermons I had dutifully kept over the last twenty-five years, and I found that Tom was right. I had been preaching the same set of Scriptures through the years, and had preached some five or six times. From that day until now I have preached from the Lectionary, and it has been a blessing to me and to our worshipping congregation.

Preach from the Bible Study Text

Bible study can sometimes be a hit-or-miss adventure, but it shouldn't be. By preaching from the same text that is used in Bible study, you allow people the opportunity to explore, meditate upon, and reflect on the text more fully before Sunday. After having the chance to ask questions, express their opinions, and ponder the text's meaning for your congregation, members bring a deeper understanding of the text to Sunday worship. They will see a bigger picture of how all the parts of worship—call to worship, prayers, music, and mission—fit together. This is an excellent way to engage members of the congregation in study and worship.

This is also a powerful way to engage those who have never been to Bible study in joining to learn more about the text being preached on Sunday. It is vital that the congregation receive the Word of God in a way that is clear, consistent, and engaging. An opportunity to learn more of the word behind the Word draws new students into Bible study.

I have been tremendously gratified by the growth of interest in Bible study. We currently offer six classes on different days and at different times during the week. The goal is to provide opportunities for as many members as possible to engage in the study of God's Word. Connecting Bible study to the Sunday message helps enhance the ability of the worshippers to access the message of the Bible that is being presented in each setting.

Preach from a Place
Other Than the Pulpit

I am a great advocate for preachers getting out of the pulpits and moving among the people. My example for this was Rev. David Durham, pastor of Mt. Sinai Baptist Church in Washington, D.C., which I joined shortly after graduating from college. Rev. Durham made the entire sanctuary into his pulpit. My earliest memories of him were of how accessible this made him to the worshippers.

So often we stay in what seems our ivory towers (the pulpit) and allow it to create a symbolic barrier or shield between the preacher and the people. A comment I have heard about contemporary worship is that the preacher moves among the people embodying the Word to the people. In some churches, the pulpit is the highest point in the physical sanctuary; it is meant to be a place of honor. But sometimes the people see the minister as above (and better than) them. It is good to break out of tradition from time to time. Come down out of the pulpit and walk among the people, preaching and teaching as you move through the aisles of the sanctuary. Be sure to have a good hand-held or lapel microphone to ensure that you are heard from wherever you are in the sanctuary. If your church is blessed to have projection screens and video cameras, be sure that the camera operator follows you so that your facial expressions can be seen. You don't want people missing parts of your sermon because they can't hear or see you! What you do want is to connect with the people, and leaving the pulpit is one way of doing that.

Preach from a Manuscript

If you preach extemporaneously or from bare-bone notes or an outline, try preaching from a manuscript. This kind of preparation allows you to craft your words and thoughts carefully. You have time to consult dictionaries and thesauruses so that you use a wider variety of words and phrases. For instance, if you want to say the sky is blue, by consulting a thesaurus you can say the sky is azure, sapphire, aquamarine, cobalt—adjectives you may not have thought of on your own. Preaching from a manuscript also allows you the time to find appropriate quotes and images. You can breathe fresh life into your sermons by reading and including appropriate poetry and quotes from plays, novels, films, and people familiar to the worshippers.

Rehearse your sermon so that you are not totally dependent on those written words. Believe me, reading your sermon is *not* the way to ignite worship. By being familiar with the manuscript, you can preach smoothly and remain open to the movement of the Holy Spirit. Dr. Samuel DeWitt Proctor was one of the greatest manuscript preachers that I have ever seen. He could bring life to the phrases on the page in ways that few others could, and his preaching style engaged the listener to want to hear more.

A manuscript provides a record of your preaching, and you will be able to see if you are preaching the same kind of sermon on the same themes. You have tangible evidence of what you are doing, and you can determine what adjustments you may want to make. Try to see the manuscript as a resource for the worship moment and in the larger educational scheme of the congregation. Again, don't be so tied to the manuscript that you shut off the movement of the Holy Spirit. The manuscript is a resource, not a mandate.

40

Memorize Your Sermon

By this I don't mean rote memorization without voice intonation or inflection. I mean knowing your sermon so well that you can preach it without notes. You may want to jot down your major points and quotes verbatim. But you should know your sermon so well that you do not need them.

I am impressed with ministers who memorize their sermons. A well-known Dallas preacher, the Reverend Dr. Freddie Haynes, memorizes his sermons, and he delivers them seamlessly. He is able to preach long quotes without missing a beat. His preaching ignites congregations across the country: he preaches in a rapid style that is impressive because he never looks at a note.

He maintains constant eye contact with his listeners as if he is having a conversation with them. This is a gift, but you cannot know if you possess it if you don't try!

Think about your favorite vocal performer or musician—they pour forth music from the heart and move you greatly. They do not read to you because they have memorized their lyrics and notes. You can do the same. It takes a bit of work and practice, but you will get through to your listeners—who will feel as if you are speaking just to them.

Ask the Congregation to Study the Text in Advance of Worship

Some ministers have the next week's texts in the current Sunday's worship bulletin and encourage members to study the texts in advance. We go a step beyond. We place the sermon texts in the church newsletter a month in advance. This has worked well, for it gives the congregation a preview of coming attractions. By knowing what the texts are ahead of time, members have the chance to read and study them. They may bring questions about the text to see if their questions are answered in the service. They certainly bring their impressions to worship. It can be exciting to see if the preacher shares the same perspective as the listeners.

We have a member in our church who reads the online Lectionary Commentary: *Samuel* each week to prepare for the sermon on Sunday. He and I have had marvelous conversations about my sermons and the lectionary texts, which have often helped me view the text from differing perspectives.

At the very least, the members of the congregation know what texts will be the focus of the service. They will bring their own ideas about themes and see what actually happens in the worship service.

Schedule Talkback
Sessions after Worship

A pastor I know holds a conversation about worship over a potluck supper after church twice a month. Members bring food, and they spend an hour after the service talking about what happened in worship. These talkbacks are ways to delve deeper into the Bible as well as worship. The congregation is engaged more deeply to reflect on God's Word as well as the overall worship experience. This is a chance for them to ask lingering questions, offer their own testimonies about how God is working in their lives, and dream about how the church can render service to the community and world based on God's challenges.

I was invited to preach in a local church on the Sunday before Martin Luther King Day. The theme of the service was Dr. King and how his faith inspired him in the civil rights movement. The pastor had scheduled a talkback after service that was well attended by the worshippers. This experience offered the worshippers the opportunity to explore deeper issues, far beyond the sermon or theme of the day.

The talkbacks can be especially meaningful if you and the worship team have a panel discussion or fishbowl conversation about how the service was planned based on the selected texts. This will allow the congregation to eavesdrop on your thinking and decision making. Believe me, after a short while, the congregation will be chomping at the bit to participate during the talkbacks. They will be ignited, excited, and more fully involved with worship.

Part Five

LITURGY

Christians gather in worship around God's Word,
and we respond in joyful gratitude.
We are called to celebrate the salvation story
and the message of God's saving deeds,
and we do so in a coherent fashion and order.
We must adapt the message
and the expressions of the message
for our contexts.
Attention should be given
to the language, customs, and social settings
in which we worship.

Update/Revise Your Order of Worship/Liturgy

Some churches use the same order of worship that they did fifty, seventy-five, or one hundred years ago. No one asks why things are done or why they are done in a particular order. Taking a long, hard look at your liturgy is one way to ignite your worship. Ask questions about the meaning of certain elements in worship and the order in which things are done. Seek the answers. Determine if the original reasons for the structure of worship still hold true for the congregation. What would it mean for the church to change its liturgy?

Liturgy is the communal response to God's presence in our lives. The foundation is Word and sacrament. So, what order allows us with all our diversity to hear God and rest in God's presence? The order of worship should embody the movement of God through history and is a living testimony to God's ongoing presence in our midst. It is the standardized order in which we honor God's saving acts. Through praise, prayer, thanksgiving, confession, repentance, sermon, and offering, we recall, renew, remember, and rehearse salvation history. We live the gospel story by how we order our worship. We lift up words, images, songs, and prayers to our God and seek deeper connection and communion with the Divine.

It is appropriate to examine the order of worship to see if things make sense and hold together. For instance, some congregations lift offerings before the sermon, and some do so after the sermon. Why? What theological statement are you making by where you place the offering? Where do we place congregational responses and why? If we place responsive prayers and readings early in the service, we invite people to participate in rather than observe worship. These are a few of the areas we need to examine to see if our liturgy does what we believe it should—invite people to participate in worshipping God.

It is also appropriate to ask if our worship space really speaks to who we understand God to be. Architectural styles that suited one generation may not be suitable for a different generation. We need to ask what our physical plants say about what we believe and why. It is good to ask what our sanctuary says about God and us theologically and spiritually. We may need to consult architects to determine what we can do to make our worship space more hospitable and more in line with our theological understandings of faith and life.

Some congregations let the order of service invite people to interact with each other. Some have an altar prayer, when members move to the front of the church for prayer and holding hands. Some invite persons to hug each other after prayer and give a brief blessing to each other. Some churches provide name tags so that people can identify each other easily.

If you use paper worship bulletins, you can add informational notes about the elements of the service—why things are ordered the way they are and what they mean. Leave space for worshippers to jot down notes or questions they want to explore further, and add a list of resources worshippers can refer to for more information about a particular element of worship. Artwork and graphics in the bulletin can support the theme of the service or provide inclusive pictures that speak to the value of diversity. Listen to what concerns your members and what distracts them from fully focusing on worship, and brainstorm solutions to see what might work. Have fun and be creative!

Develop Living Liturgy

We serve and belong to the Living God. Why then are our liturgies so dead? Living Liturgy is an attempt to recognize that each generation has the responsibility of linking the past and the present with an eye to the future. Worship is contextual; you need to consider your local context in order to create opportunities for vibrant worship that honors roots (past) and wings (future).

The liturgy does double duty, reminding members of God's love and grace and inviting persons to join the fellowship. How we shape worship and the space within which we worship can reveal what we really think about God, ourselves, and all of creation. The liturgy, therefore, should not be static and fixed. Rather it should allow for changing realities while holding to core traditions, values, convictions, and hopes. The Living God continues to speak to us in ways that hold meaning and purpose for us. Our liturgies should reflect the timelessness of God's presence and movement throughout creation.

Thus, liturgy should reflect the realities of changing language, customs, cultural awareness, and historical conditions and situations. We are called to respond fully to God's presence through our liturgical elements. Toward this end, we must pay attention to how we talk about God. For example, inclusive language is the norm in many churches these days; we should not limit our images of God to masculine descriptions. Likewise, we must be careful not to use racist, sexist, ageist, or homophobic language and images in our liturgies. God extends extravagant welcome to all, and our liturgies should reflect comprehensive inclusiveness. This also means that children and youth are integral parts of the body of Christ. Every effort should be made to make all feel welcome, valued, and affirmed through our liturgies.

In addition to extending lavish welcome and hospitality, our liturgies should point to greater service to the world. This means that we care about all of creation—human, plant, animal, and all forms of life. Because we care, we extend ourselves and commit to acts of justice. Our liturgies should challenge and encourage us to stand on the side of justice in all matters.

Our liturgies should speak to the whole person, which means worship should appeal to all the senses. Our worship services should include opportunities to use our heads, hearts, hands, and feet. Thus, we are concerned about music, movement, and the full participation of persons in worship.

The Bible is used in the liturgical life of congregations through movement, song, prayer, and educational opportunities. Biblical passages are the foundations for prayers, calls to worship, rituals, sacramental elements, benedictions, and the like. The more we pay attention to these liturgical elements, the better we are assured that our liturgy reflects who God is and who we are. We are challenged to celebrate the fullness of the message of God's saving deeds—now and forever more—by what we do and why!

Wear Bright-Colored Robes

When I graduated from seminary, the standard pulpit fare was a white robe for Communion Sundays and black for the rest of the year. The thought was that modesty in vestments would allow the congregation to focus on God and not the minister. I pretty much felt the same way: the black robe was the uniform for clergy, and every minister I knew had a black robe. When women entered the ministry in substantial numbers, they rebelled against the uniform and opted for more colorful robes. I'm sure they met some resistance at first. But the more people saw the red robes, purple robes, yellow robes, they realized that the colors added a jazzy element to the standard, and they liked it.

In addition to the change brought by women, ministers—male and female—began to dress more in custom with their culture. Ministers began wearing robes more in line with their indigenous garb—kente cloth, silk—as an expression of their culture.

Colorful garb for worship is a nice way of injecting something different and dramatic. Also, colorful robes are not just for the preachers. More and more churches are opting for colorful robes for their choirs.

Don't Wear Robes

Some ministers are saying no to robes . . . period. The men preach in suits, and women preach in dresses or suits. Such choices blur the separation between clergy and laity. All are worshippers together. Clothing is no longer a barrier to authentic community worship.

Even choirs are forgoing robes. Some churches already discard their robes during the warm summer months in facilities that do not have central air. Some require members to dress in similar colors (for example, white shirts and blouses and navy or black slacks or skirts). Some choirs are dressing in culturally specific garb that celebrate their ethnicity.

For both preacher and choirs, a freedom comes when robes are set aside. All are equal in worship, and clothes do not mark worship leaders from those in the pew. It is a refreshing change to be oneself in worship. Clothing choices indicate the level of formality for worship. Casting off robes signals that we are gathered to have a good time and are not hindered by concerns for how our expressive actions affect our clothes. In addition, without robes, worship leaders are free to move without dishonoring the robe or office to which the robe points.

Dress in Casual/Sports Clothing

Every church needs services where the folk can come as they are! There is a popular activity that some neighborhoods sponsor: the Come as You are Party. The hosts send ambassadors door-to-door: "There's a cookout at the Joneses in fifteen minutes and you are invited! No need to dress up or prepare anything—just come as you are."

What a wonderful idea for the church to consider. In some cultures, dressing up for church is seen as a way to honor God; after all, we want to present ourselves to God in the best possible light. It's like dating; we want our intended to have no excuse to reject us, so we always strive to look our best. But what if that doesn't matter to God? What if God wants us to present our real selves—without the makeup, fancy haircuts, and hairdos, without the shined shoes and fancy pumps? What if God wants us to show up just as we are?

It is surprising what informal clothing does to ignite worship. I started a Saturday evening worship service in addition to the Sunday morning worships. We publicized the Saturday worship service as a come-as-you are service. I modeled this for the members—showing up one week in jeans, the next in sweatshirt and sneakers, the next in a suit because I had just left officiating a wedding. The members soon got the point that they could wear comfortable clothing—and they felt freer to praise God without worrying about messing up their clothes or their hair or their shoes. We were all able to relax and have a good time praising and worshipping God.

Make Communion More Meaningful

Communion, or the celebration of the Lord's Supper, is an important element in Christian worship. It is a time of remembering Jesus' last days with his disciples and the meal they shared together before his arrest and crucifixion. The Communion story is filled with drama, and we should find ways to create anticipation for the shared meal. Many Communion liturgies begin with an invitation to the table and close with a prayer of thanksgiving. You can invite the congregation to sing a hymn specifically designated for Communion either before or after the invitation. Many congregations sing hymns during the sharing of the bread and wine, such as "Let Us Break Bread Together."

The point is to make Communion an event. It is a ritual of the church that signals something will be different after it occurs. For us Christians, it is a renewal of our commitment to God through Jesus Christ. As often as we eat and drink, we remember Christ, who is God with us, and the ongoing flow of grace, mercy, and love from God. We are guests at God's table; we come to the table to be refreshed, fed, nourished, and fortified for the journey ahead.

Communion offers the opportunity to explore cultural diversity. What would it mean for your congregation to use rice and sake in place of bread and wine? Or corn bread and Kool-Aid? Or tortillas and lemonade? Or an agape meal of crackers, breads, and fruits? We commemorate Christ's sacrifice at the Communion meal. This is no empty ritual; it is a real meal with the risen Christ and is a foretaste of the heavenly banquet over which Christ will preside at the end of history. In the breaking of the bread and the sharing of the cup, in whatever cultural forms they take, we remember that we are one in the body of Christ, the church, and we make known that all are welcome to the table.

A pastor friend of mine does something unique. Once a year, instead of preaching a regular sermon on Communion Sunday, she teaches the Communion story. While the biblical narrative gets highlighted during Lent, she chooses an additional time of the church season to teach the texts to the congregation, reminding them of what Communion meant to the disciples and what it means for us today, whatever our context may be. Her parishioners express appreciation for the reminder—it keeps Communion from becoming an empty ritual. Instead, it becomes an opportunity to express thanksgiving as well as an extravagant welcome inviting all to the table. It also serves to remind members that we live in hope of sitting at God's banquet table at the close of history. Communion lends itself well to dramatic readings, the acting out of the Scripture, poetic images, and dramatic space design and decoration.

Make Baptism / Baby Dedication More Meaningful

Like Communion, baptisms and baby dedications are rituals of the church that deserve more attention. Through the ritual of baptism, persons join the body of Christ and walk in newness of life. Such an event is momentous in the life of the person being baptized and in the life of the congregation. Create a mini-worship service around baptism, using appropriate Scripture and including congregational singing and responsive prayers and litanies. Involve the congregation as much as possible. In the midst of Sunday worship, we witness to and celebrate the baptism of those who accept God's invitation into God's household, and we welcome them to the family.

And don't be afraid to dramatize the rite of baptism—the story is conducive to it. In fact, baptism is one of the more dramatic moments in the life of a Christian. This ritual creates a new person, a child of God, who emerges from the water changed and new—now belonging to the body of Christ.

For baby dedications, you can include parents, grandparents, godparents, and all who will commit to raising the child. A litany of commitment to be a strong and spiritual presence in the life of the child is appropriate. A well-known African proverb states that it takes a village to raise a child; the entire congregation can be the village! It is important to create and use a liturgy especially for this occasion.

You may want to preach a sermon series on baptism, telling the history of baptism from the Hebrew Bible (Old Testament) and its continuing significance in the Christian Scripture (New Testament), Jesus' encounter with John the Baptist, Jesus' baptism, and the importance of baptism in the letters and ministry of Paul. Baptism presents prime opportunities for teaching moments that educate and edify members of all ages.

Part Six

TECHNOLOGY

Technology is a tool that can enhance and enliven worship.
New forms of communication can make the difference
between a church that is alive and one that is stagnant.
Don't be intimidated by technology.
Explore how it can work for your congregational worship.

Make Sound Pleasing to the Ear

This point speaks to acoustics, furniture arrangement, and function, and requires some thought. What would make sound more pleasing in your worship space? Do you have more than one space used for worship? For instance, you may use the sanctuary except in the summer when you may use a more informal space. What does each space require to meet the needs of those gathered? The pipe organ might be just fine for the large sanctuary, but you may need amplifiers and synthesizers in the fellowship hall for informal worship services. What kind of sound system is better suited for instruments other than organ or piano?

A good sound system provides the versatility you need for different kinds of services and different styles of worship. You don't want music and speech to be too soft or too loud; you'll lose people either way. I have been through the fire and the flood with this one. It is often hard to get the point across to those who lead music and worship that the sound is too soft or too loud or too caustic. The message must be communicated, if sound is to be used effectively and beneficially in worship.

In Christian churches in the Middle Ages, antiphonal singing was developed. Choirs would sing from the back and front of the sanctuary, to provide a unique and different experience for the listener. Today many churches are opting for surround sound rather than placing all speakers in the front of the sanctuary. Quality sound can enhance worship in ways that elevate the worshippers to new spiritual levels.

Utilize Creative and Adequate Lighting

Many of our churches are like dark caves because the lighting is inadequate for today's worship services. Dim lights may have been fine for worship in Gothic structures but are not conducive to vibrant worship, especially for those of us who live in the Snow Belt where we have disproportionately more cloudy days than other parts of the country. We have many dreary days each year with little natural light and hardly ever see sunshine in the fall and winter. In addition to moving furniture around and creating beautiful sanctuary spaces, you can add lighting to help set the tone and atmosphere for worship.

Consult a lighting designer to help you think through what kinds of lighting you want. For instance, you may want spotlights to highlight musical or vocal soloists, softer lights with color jellies to serve as background for liturgical dancers, dimmer lights to set a mood for contemplative prayer, bright lights to emit energy for lively music, or good pulpit and lectern lights to make sure worship leaders have adequate light when they are reading.

Some lighting solutions can be inexpensive while others require longer-range planning. Remember that lighting is affected by paint color on the walls, worship space furniture, the color and texture of any drapery in the space, stained-glass windows, the number of doors leading into the space, and so on. But don't be intimidated: ask for help and use light effectively.

Install Projection Screens

Projection screens are a tremendous blessing to twenty-first century worship. They enable the church to save money on printing bulletins and purchasing music. They allow for enormous creativity during worship from projecting those who lead worship, to highlighting Scripture texts, to illustrating sermon points with vivid scenes and video. There is no limit to what can be done with projection screens. They are an investment that pays for itself in igniting your worship.

There is a Japanese United Church of Christ congregation in northern California whose former youth ministry intern made great use of technology. He used a projection screen on two special occasions. The first was to show videos that the youth had taken when interviewing the elders of the church. It was moving to see and hear the young people ask questions about the elders' past: What events stand out for them, in what ways had God moved in their lives, what lessons do they wish to leave for younger generations? The youth ministry intern helped the youth develop interview questions, videotaped the interviews, and helped the youth edit their work. The video is part of the church's history and was buried in a time capsule to be opened in fifty years.

The second occasion was to show a slideshow of highlights of a youth retreat. The photos were candid shots of the weekend's time away. There were photos of sunrise worship services, mealtimes, pool time, sports, Bible study; the photos serve as a chronicle of the event as well as reminders that youth know how to create spaces where they meet the Divine. Both of these presentations allowed the entire church to be participants in something where they may not have been physically present.

There are a multitude of other uses for projection screens. By posting weekly church and community announcements before the worship service begins, you give those who gather early an opportunity to see what events are coming up. You can post the order of service and eliminate the need for paper bulletins. One church I know tried this, however, and soon had to produce a small number of bulletins to be sent to the sick and shut in. The pastor also learned that several members sent bulletins to friends and relatives who lived in other cities. This knowledge helped the pastor engage the congregation in an evangelism program that energized the people—an unexpected benefit of taking the risk to do something different and new.

Projection screens can be used to provide the lyrics to new songs, to illustrate mission events, to share messages from the denomination. . . . Let your imagination soar as you explore ways to engage your congregation in the use of technology.

A CLOSING WORD

We have explored fifty-two ways to ignite your worship—practical, hands-on suggestions that have been tried and tested. You may incorporate all of these suggestions or test a few and evaluate.

Remember that your congregational liturgy includes the order of worship, language, hospitality, architecture, music, leadership, mission and service, theology, and community—and much, much more. Allow times in the worship service for exuberant expression, celebration and contemplation, stillness and movement, drama and pageantry, listening and speaking. Appeal to all the senses and be open to the movement of the Holy Spirit. We gather as a gifted community, offering our gifts in praise of our God who loves us and accepts us. We belong to God and to each other; our liturgies should reflect that.

As with anything we do in church, you want to set aside some significant time to review the changes you've made and evaluate their effectiveness. Many churches are reluctant to evaluate their congregational life, but there is nothing to fear about taking an honest look at what you do, why you do it, and what you can do to improve your worship life.

Some questions you might consider as you assess your worship include but are not limited to

• What is your favorite part of the worship service? Why?

• What do you find distracting in worship?

- What are your favorite hymns, anthems, songs? Why do these hold meaning for you?

- What would help you surrender to the worship experience?

- What worship themes and sermons have been most meaningful for you? Why?

- What one or two elements about worship would you like to see changed? Changed to what?

- What element of worship do you most look forward to? What element do you wish were eliminated?

- What do you share with others about your church's worship services?

Through our prayers, worship, and sacraments, we rehearse God's gracious acts and celebrate God's love, grace, and mercy toward us. Let us remember that vibrant, energetic, life-giving worship is the work of all God's people. Worship, *leitourgia*, is the calling of every Christian and every congregation. We offer our worship to God, not to ourselves. We *all* must live our lives grounded in the life, ministry, death, and resurrection of Jesus Christ and be ever open to the movement of God's Holy Spirit. Blessings!

SELECTED RESOURCES

Alves, Elizabeth. *Becoming a Prayer Warrior: A Guide to Effective and Powerful Prayer.* Ventura, Calif. Regal, 2003.

Bass, Dorothy C. (editor). *Practicing Our Faith: A Way of Life for a Searching People.* San Francisco: Jossey-Bass, 2010.

Book of Worship: United Church of Christ. New York: Office for Church Life and Leadership, 1986.

Costen, Melva Wilson. *African American Christian Worship.* Nashville: Abingdon Press, 1993.

deWaal Malefyt, Norma, and Howard Vanderwell. *Designing Worship Together: Models and Strategies for Worship Planning.* Herndon, Va.: Alban Institute, 2005.

Emerson, Michael O., with Rodney M. Woo. *People of the Dream: Multiracial Congregations in the United States.* Princeton, N.J.: Princeton University Press, 2006.

González, Justo L. (editor). *¡Alabadle! Hispanic Christian Worship.* Nashville: Abingdon, 1996.

———, and Pablo A. Jiménez, *Púlpito: An Introduction to Hispanic Preaching.* Nashville: Abingdon, 2005.

Hawn, Michael. *One Bread, One Body: Exploring Cultural Diversity in Worship.* Herndon, Va.: Alban Institute, 2003.

Kapp, Deborah J. *Worship Frames: How We Shape and Interpret Our Experience of God.* Herndon, Va.: Alban Institute, 2008.

Kim, Eunjoo Mary. *Preaching the Presence of God: A Homiletic from an Asian American Perspective.* Valley Forge, Pa. Judson Press, 1999.

Long, Thomas G. *Beyond the Worship Wars: Building Vital and Faithful Worship.* Herndon, Va.: Alban Institute, 2001.

Lord, Jennifer. *Finding Language and Imagery: Words for Holy Speech (Elements of Preaching).* Minneapolis: Fortress Press, 2010.

Mitchell, Henry H. *Celebration and Experience in Preaching.* Rev. ed. Nashville: Abingdon, 2008.

Sadler, Paul Hobson. *Walk in the Light: Insight and Reflections on Living the Christian Life.* Shaker Heights, Ohio: Creative Arts Ministries, Inc. 1998

Sing! Prayer and Praise. Cleveland: Pilgrim Press, 2009.

Songs of Zion: Supplemental Worship Resources. 12. Nashville: Abingdon Press, 1981.

Stewart, Carlyle Fielding, III. *African American Church Growth: 12 Principles for Prophetic Ministry.* Nashville: Abingdon Press, 1994.

Taylor, Barbara Brown. *The Preaching Life.* Cambridge, Mass.: Cowley Publications, 1993.

Thurman, Howard. *Disciplines of the Spirit.* Richmond, Ind.: Friends United Press, 1977.

Walker, James R. *Lakota Belief and Ritual.* Lincoln: Bison Books/University of Nebraska Press, 1991.